ADOLESCENCE AND BREAKDOWN

edited by
Simon Meyerson
Senior Psychologist, North Middlesex Hospital
Consultant Psychologist, Quaesitor, London

Foreword by
Dr Robert Gosling
Senior Psychoanalyst, Consultant Psychiatrist, Chairman,
Professional Committee, Tavistock Clinic

London · George Allen & Unwin Ltd
Ruskin House · Museum Street

First published in 1975

© George Allen & Unwin Ltd. 1975

ISBN 0 04 150053 9 hardback
0 04 150054 7 paperback

Printed in Great Britain
by Willmer Brothers Limited
Birkenhead.

FOREWORD

In *Adolescence* an attempt has been made to describe some of the salient features of the adolescent and his world. Erikson[1] has identified the central psychological challenge of the adolescent as the development and maintenance of fidelity. In so far as this is a never-ending challenge, although it may later be overshadowed by other psychological demands, it remains a hazard and liable to disruption. To the extent that this is so, breakdowns of one sort or another in later life may well be little different in their main features from disturbances encountered in adolescence. Of course such breakdown will look very different because of intervening biological maturation, psychological learning and elaboration, and changes in social circumstances. But if a failure in faithfulness, whether to people or ideals, is what has taken place, it will be the anguish that is peculiar to adolescence that recurs.

Obviously developmental achievements prior to adolescence may also be lost temporarily in later breakdowns. Erikson describes these as the achievements of coherence in being, of the capacity for hope, trust and confidence, of the ability to assert will and purpose and the achievement of competence. Any of these achievements, if none too well established, will be the first to go under stressful experiences in later life. The loss of some of them may well be the leading feature of a disturbance of development during adolescence as it may in later episodes. But to the extent that the newly developing capacity for fidelity is what is at hazard, the troubled times of an adolescent are special.

When the pains of the adolescent or of his environment exceed a certain point the helping professions are sometimes mobilised. Some sort of breakdown has occurred. In *Adolescence and Breakdown* Simon Meyerson has assembled the deliberations of a number of his colleagues who have been so used. They inevitably give a rather lugubrious or frightening picture of adolescent experience and by the nature of their preoccupation talk little about all that is well. A less one-sided picture is presented by many of the same authors in *Adolescence.*[2] But here they tell us about how things can go wrong, when this has happened, various kinds of help can be offered.

Such studies can in the tradition of much clinical investigation indicate to us what the developmental processes are that have failed or come to grief. Knowledge about development is thereby increased and more rational measures for intervening suggested. But in addition, those chiefly concerned with breakdowns in later life may learn a lot just by being shown some processes in purer culture than they are ever likely to see.

Robert Gosling
Tavistock Clinic
April 1974

REFERENCES

1. E. H. Erikson, *Insight and Responsibility* (London, Faber, 1964).

2. The companion volume *Adolescence: The Crises of Adjustment* is referred to as *Adolescence* throughout this book for the sake of brevity.

About the Authors

BILL ALLCHIN is Consultant Psychiatrist and Psychotherapist at Leigh House Adolescent Unit at Chandler's Ford and at Southampton Child and Family Guidance Clinic.

JOHN BYNG-HALL is Consultant Psychiatrist to the Department of Children and Parents, Tavistock Clinic and Camden Assessment Centre.

MARTYN GAY is a Consultant Child Psychiatrist and is Clinical Teacher in Mental Health at Bristol University. Previously he was Senior Registrar at the Royal Hospital for Sick Children in Edinburgh.

ARTHUR HYATT WILLIAMS is a Senior Psychoanalyst, Consultant Psychiatrist and Chairman of the Adolescent Department, Tavistock Clinic. He is the visiting Psychotherapist to Wormwood Scrubs.

SHIONA J. HYATT WILLIAMS has worked in infant welfare, maternity and family planning clinics and is Medical Officer at Sussex University.

SIMON MEYERSON is Senior Psychologist at the North Middlesex Hospital and is a Group Therapist at Quaesitor, London. Previously he was Senior Psychologist at the Tavistock Institute and the Adolescent Department of the Tavistock Clinic.

BRIAN MUIR is Head of the Department of Adolescent and Family Psychiatry at the Cassel Hospital. He is also a psychoanalyst and consultant psychiatrist.

ARTURO VARCHEVKER is a psychiatrist and has worked with adolescents both at the Tavistock and at a variety of hospitals, including the Henderson, Cassel and Marlborough Day.

CONTENTS

1

Problems of Adolescence

A. HYATT WILLIAMS

Classification is difficult because there are several scales, ranges or dimensions present in each individual. The adolescent is growing up in at least one, and usually several, social groupings. He brings to the multitudinous problems which are centred round puberty the psychosocial problems derived from the other social groupings which complicate the issue of adolescent development. Each action carried out in the present is based upon the past and materially influences the future.

Looking with hindsight as the history unfolds, one can discern the way in which sequences of events could have been forecast without any special ability or omniscience. With experience, how often it appears that such predictions can be made in advance. There is always the unexpected, however, which arises from within the individual, or externally from one social grouping or another. Sometimes it occurs in the wider environmental field and vitally influences the adolescent. An example of the first is when some sudden internal psychic shift takes place and the once-diligent pre-pubertal pupil becomes the 'drop-out' student of the next decade. An example of the second cause is the fatal illness and death of a member of the nuclear family. An example of the third is a catastrophe such as an air-crash, flood, motor accident or even a crime of violence which impinges upon the individual at risk in so massive a way that emotional digestion and metabolism cannot keep pace with the over-whelming stress of the moment.

The child at the end of the latency period is relatively well adapted to his environment. He has become skilled in a whole variety of ways. For example, as a pedestrian in both rural and urban settings he has become remarkably safe and reliable. Formal knowledge is being acquired and a lot of it integrated at a fairly fast rate, although such initiation tests as the eleven-plus sometimes put the latency child into consider-able disarray. The prescribed position in which the adolescent finds himself within the family group has usually reached some degree of stability by the end of the latency period. Then with varying degrees of suddenness, puberty with its biological changes breaks and all the secondary turmoil which constitutes the adolescent process follows sequentially in an infinitely variable way. Beneath all this variable super-structure, which at times is confusing to the adolescent him-self, and also to the people who have to deal with him, is a substructure of invariability. How do we study the interaction between the variables and the invariables?

Adolescence is the period of experiencing and resolving the turbulence which is set into action by the biological process of puberty. Change in size and status within the home and in the wider environment are not the least of these. Adolescence ends with the beginning of adult life. Adoles-cence therefore is the consequence of puberty and the extent to which it taxes the adaptive capacities of the young person varies from culture to culture and also depends to some extent upon the biological acuteness of the onset of puberty. The first way of looking at adolescent problems therefore is to see how the individual is put under stress and how his adaptive capacities are able to cope with the various chal-lenges. Sometimes the main difficulties are experienced as being situated at home within the nuclear family, sometimes at school, college, university or place of work, and some-times elsewhere. Any interactive situation is liable to be designated as the cause of the difficulty, so that the real stress situation may not become clearly discernible until preliminary sorting out has been undertaken. It may well be that some of the sorting out can be conducted by non-medical agencies and this is the value of the counselling services for young people. As in childhood where the help of parents is sought and instant remedies often found possible, so the adolescent seeks for help from authorities including parents, schoolteachers and others. Rarely are such instant remedies and solutions to problems—such as those effective in the former childhood difficulties—possible in the case of adolescent problems. The young person at this juncture often becomes disillusioned and angry with the helping authority, blames it for not helping more, and designates it as being punitive and useless. This is one of the common causes of the alienation of adolescents from even helpful and benign authority and the inevitable drift is towards a peer group for mutual comfort and understanding. Sometimes the peer group is sought for more disturbed and destructive activities such as revenge upon authority or the easy options of drink, drug-taking, etc. Sometimes the peer group is only minimally alienated from society at large and may, in certain respects, be a good deal more constructive and far-sighted than the society against which it is in rebellion. Again there is a spectrum or scale. At the severely disturbed and alienated end there is delinquency, drug-taking and behaviour which seems to be orientated more towards death than life.

So far we have been considering adaptation and the stresses to which the adaptive capacities of the adolescent are subjected. No mention has been made of psychological illness. A point may be reached, however, beyond which, if stresses continue or are increased, adaptive capacities are overwhelmed.

The problem is very confused and complicated because the overwhelming of the adaptive capacities may result in a definitive illness on the one hand or there may be a character distortion, for example in the direction of delinquency, or there may be a reduction in achievement. Most often, however, there are mixtures of these three and also there are other kinds of response. For example, one fifteen-year-old boy responded to the desertion of the family by his beloved

13

father by poor scholastic performance, by fire-setting and also by turning to very destructive, aggressive and sexual behaviour towards young children of either sex, including his own siblings. He was not a talker but a doer. Eventually, when it was possible to get him to speak he gave as his reason for the behaviour, which utterly disregarded the rights and satisfactory development of a young girl, that he did not care what the effect upon her was although he did not dislike her. When asked to explain why this was so, he said immediately and with much feeling, 'My father did not think of the effect on me of his leaving home and my never seeing him.'

Adolescent disturbances and breakdown patterns are similar to those of adults in that they take place along the lines of personality cleavage which were laid down during the earlier phases of emotional development. The fixation points referred to in *Adolescence*, Chapter 1, constitute the weaknesses or cleavage lines which are especially vulnerable to later stress situations. These situations may consist of what is going on in the inner world, that is intraphysically, or in the outer world, that is psychosocially. Or they may be due to disturbances of the body image due to illness or other damage to the body including delusions about the body. What is different about the disturbances of adolescents from those of adults is the instability of the whole situation. Nothing is fixed and all feelings are powerfully represented so that turbulence is maximal. Also there can be rapid shifts from a wise and seemingly adult intellectual understanding to a rage or panic-driven state like that of a young child in a wild tantrum.

Particularly characteristic of disturbed adolescents is the way in which individual distress tends to be expressed in group relationships based upon the externalisation of blame and responsibility. In this case the goodness is usually ascribed to the adolescent in-group and the badness to the adult world outside. Particularly singled out for hostility, of course, is the police force. In general, adolescent disturbance consists of too much yielding to instincts, acting-out, delinquency, promiscuity, etc. But also there can be too much inhibition of instincts, inactivity, indolence, inability to hold a job, inability to study and the restrictive neurotic disturbances. If the ego structure is too flimsy the adolescent personality seems unable to contain the powerful forces which reside within it. On the other hand, too harsh a superego or persecuting conscience leads not only to inhibition but may lead to a great increase of internal tension and subsequently a major outbreak in the form perhaps of antisocial behaviour or of suicide or suicidal attempt. Much depends upon the identifications. In general, the adolescent may be a conformist and identify with the authority in which case he is likely to be prudish, perhaps arrogant, smug, complacent and in general 'holier than thou'. On the other hand he may identify with the underdog and the authority becomes designated as the enemy to be torn down however good it is. A third way of dealing with problems is to form part of a delinquent subculture. Sometimes the delinquency constitutes a subculture within the personality of the individual so that at home, at school, at university or even at work, he is a perfect conformist and gives no trouble but at the same time within his peer group leads a secret delinquent life. The recent escalation of drug taking facilitates this kind of split.

One of the greatest difficulties with which the adolescent may have to cope is when the authority figures, parents especially, are corrupt. This means that when, by introjection, projection and reintrojection occurring repeatedly in the formation of the superego, criminal corrupt authorities form important ingredients or constituents of the conscience of the individual. Of course, this kind of happening takes place much earlier in life than adolescence and is important long before puberty is reached. But it is during the adolescent phase that it assumes new importance. This is partly because of the increased stresses acting upon the adolescent and partly because of his greater impact upon his social and cultural environment. He is more mobile and delinquent action is likely to have wider repercussions. The condition of having superego figures who are corrupt is serious because in circumstances in which ordinary people can obtain help and guidance from their moral but not too punitive superegos, corrupt superego figures are unreliable, capricious,

15

sometimes allowing delinquencies and sometimes forbidding arbitrarily non-delinquent behaviour. At worst, there is a sneering at the good side of the adolescent, and the encouragement or the acquiescence over the delinquent side. Sometimes a hostile parent deliberately corrupts or an envious relative encourages the destructive and brutalised aspects of the young person. An example from literature is the way in which Heathcliff in *Wuthering Heights* corrupted the young Earnshaw, and another example of the opposite kind is in *Treasure Island* where Long John Silver made no serious attempt to corrupt Jim Hawkins.

Seduction during childhood can influence maladjustment at adolescence. Freud made reference to the seduction in childhood of both a real and a fantasy nature and concluded that although actual seduction was common, a great deal was contributed by the fantasies of the child. Nevertheless, seductions do take place and these can be seen to fall roughly into the categories of threats to life and threats to the integrity of the body. The other kind of traumatic event is the seduction which is frightening but stimulating. Whether seduction occurs with excitement and cruelty or whether it occurs with excitement and kindness, the result seems to be little different. The excitement and cruelty seems to trigger off a tendency in the person who was seduced as a child to do actively to other people representing himself as he then was what he or she experienced passively in childhood. Excitement linked with kindness tends to perpetuate the distortion involved in the original seductive relationship; for example, to perpetuate a homosexual object choice or various sexually perverse practices. Whichever way we look upon the problem, it is certainly true to say that the basic pattern of behaviour, of personality development and of attitude to life, is laid down early on in personal development. It would be fair to say that constitution and heredity are basic but that the actual events of life and actual experiences also contribute a great deal. An example of the effects of trauma during a state of persecutory anxiety would be a relatively minor seduction which is experienced by the individual child as an extraordinary, malevolent, cruel and destructive event leaving an indelible effect upon him and causing him to live from then on with a sense of grievance and to feel that, having been wronged, he is quite entitled to perpetuate wrongs wherever he goes for the rest of his life.

In trying to understand the perplexing morass of adolescent turbulence it is important to look for guide lines. Some of these were described in *Adolescence,* Chapter 1. They will be recapitulated briefly and slightly differently here. According to the theories of Klein and her co-workers, the emotional development of the infant was stated to proceed from a phase dominated by persecutory anxiety which consists of a fear of attack, even to the point of annihilation, by malevolent agencies, experienced at this phase as part-objects. This means that the infant experiences a persecutory breast, not a bad mother. The depressive position is described by Klein as that phase which is initiated by the recognition by the baby of the mother as a person, rather than as a collection of parts. The hostile feelings which the baby had experienced and expressed towards the bad breast (a part-object) and the loving and grateful feelings felt towards the good gratifying breast (still part-object) come together in relationship to a whole mother, with both kinds of attributes. Depressive anxiety arises due to concern for the good object and of fear lest the hostile destructive feelings should be more powerful than the loving ones. On that account, there is a risk that the whole mother will be driven away or destroyed. This experience constitutes a change and a development. Depressive anxiety involves feelings of concern and responsibility. Persecutory anxiety involves only feelings of fear and aggrievedness. If the depressive position is worked through to some extent in infancy, the baby is able to extend and deepen its relationships. These relationships are first with its mother, experienced as a whole person, and then with father and then with other people. Normally there is some negotiation of the depressive position and it may be some time before an inadequate negotiation of the depressive position is recognised. The signs of this will be shown in various intrapsychic and psychosocial difficulties in the course of the development of the young child. In all people, however, there

17

are constant relapses into states dominated by persecutory anxiety, however well the depressive position has been negotiated in infancy. At the end of the scale which is dominated by depressive anxiety, there can be growth, development and a capacity for the unconscious adaptive process known as sublimation. People, represented intrapsychically by images (often called internal objects in this book) are tolerated and there is an on-going relationship with them. The intrapsychic or inner world of the individual and the interpersonal or social world with other people can be kept in some sort of working relationship and for short periods of time even in harmony. In favourable states which are dominated by depressive anxiety, a good deal of unconscious psychic work is done. This means that the inner world of fantasy of the individual is used as a valuable testing-out ground, and valuable steps in integration and maturation. Violent turning away from the breast, from the mother, and from all other persons who are felt to be frustrating is characteristic of the paranoid/schizoid phase of emotional development. This is the phase which is dominated by persecutory anxiety. The persecutory response to the deprivation of weaning is characterised by a violent turning away from the breast or bottle. It usually lays down a pattern of behaviour which is repeated on every occasion in life where there is a loss or separation from either good objects or those gratifications which are felt to be necessary by the individual. I feel that the influence of early infancy on later maladjustment cannot be overstated:

1. The kind of turning away from the breast or bottle is likely to be typical of later responses to frustration or deprivation.

2. The more violent the turning away from the primal object, i.e. breast-bottle and later mother, the more unlikely it is that there was much success in reaching and working through the depressive position, and individuals of this kind tend to express their difficulties and distress in deeds rather than being able to do the work within their

minds until the situation has, to some extent, been improved.

3. It is the latter category of people from whom maladjusted individuals, criminals and delinquents are largely recruited.

A Way of Assessing Adolescent Problems: The Personality Profile

As has been stated already, breakdowns and illnesses which occur during the period of adolescence are difficult to classify as they are due to an interplay of factors and usually, therefore, cannot be regarded as disease entities. Possibly a more useful way of assessing the adolescent who is referred for one reason or another to the health or the other caring services would be to look at the disturbance in the setting of the total personality of the individual, and then to consider the individual in his various social settings, beginning with the nuclear family and continuing with the school, university or work setting, etc. In this way a personality profile can be looked at and the areas of disability evaluated. There can be a classification without loss of the overall integrative picture of the whole individual.

With the aim of facilitating the study of the disturbed adolescent who has been referred or who has brought himself or herself for help of one kind or another, a diagrammatic chart or grid has been drawn out. The one which is given at the end of this chapter is crude, may not be suitable, and certainly needs modification by individual workers who are attempting to look at adolescent persons who have to be seen in a meaningful way. The principles involved in such a scheme are simple. The aim is to present graphically the kinds of disturbance, the areas and phases of development from whence they stem, their significance in the total picture of the personality of the individual involved, their intensity, and their relationship to the contemporary functioning of the individual. In addition it will be quite clear when the schema is looked at that it will not be filled in completely for every

19

PERSONALITY PROFILE

INTENSITY OF STRESS FACTORS:

Constitutional, Historical, Environmental Factors:	(Assets) working smoothly	Under stress (Reversible)	Over-whelmed (break-down)	Irreversible by change of circumstance only	Definitive illness	Personality disorder, neurotic, psychotic, delinquent	Gross limitation of capacity	Kind of anxiety	Other reactions:
HEREDITY AND CONSTITUTION									
INTELLIGENCE									
INDULGENCE									
DEPRIVATION									
SEPARATION									
SEDUCTION									
ILLNESS ACCIDENT									
FAMILY CONSTELLATION									
SOCIAL RELATIONS									
ATTITUDE TO LIFE									
OTHER FACTORS:									
CAPACITY TO CHANGE:									
RESPONSE TO HELP:									

OVERALL SUMMARY

adolescent referral. The schema acts as an *aide-mémoire* so that important areas of the personality are not neglected and can be run over by the worker so that no major factor is omitted.

The vertical categories deal with heredity and environmental factors and then go on to later impositions such as separation, illness and various traumatic happenings. The horizontal column denotes mainly intensity and the way in which the various stress factors have been dealt with or woven into distortions and disabilities of character. I would suggest that a five-point index of quantity or intensity be used, either 1,2,3,4,5 or A,B,C,D,E, but there is no reason why a descriptive word or phrase should not be put in any given box. There are spaces for the inclusion of special individual factors. Finally there is space at the end for short summaries involving a sentence or two. It must be stressed that the schema has nothing particularly magical about it and it should be modified, cast aside or totally replaced by something which works better for the individual who wishes to use this kind of schema. If we try to use the grid for one or two actual patients, the point of it might become clearer.

P.L. was a sixteen-year-old, well-built boy from a tropical country, whose parents referred him in collaboration with the school where he was a boarder, on account of his academic failure and apparent boredom. The scale will show how the trouble can be located in the area of intellectual capacity and traced to birth trauma consisting of rather prolonged anoxia. The mother was asked about the birth of her son, who was her eldest child, and stated that she had been in labour for three days and then had to have an emergency Caesarean operation. The doctors at the time were concerned about the prolonged anoxia and thought it must have a profoundly deleterious effect upon the intelligence and future development of the baby. The other children in that particular family were all of very high intelligence. The boredom of P.L. was explained as a withdrawal, partly defensive, against very primitive anxieties and partly because so many things were going on at school which he could not cope with, and once he lost the trend could not pick up again. The hope was that he would be able to learn with special tuition up to a modest level of achievement and that this in his own cultural environment would be quite adequate as long as he did not get himself involved in higher administration, politics or confronted by complicated open-ended problems. The parents had to get used to the idea that their only son and eldest child would not be able to reach their level of distinction, but was quite capable of leading a satisfactory life. It will be seen that not many of the compartments need be filled, but it can be fairly easy to see the outlines of this case.

C.R. was a handsome twenty-year-old man, the youngest of four in his family, who had passed 'O' and 'A' levels with distinction. In his final year at a provincial university he had become a drop-out, being unable to study and afraid to sit out the hours of the final examination in the room with all the other candidates. He had had to leave early with an almost phobic urgency. His history, particularly his childhood history, was apparently without traumatic event. Early trauma and separation had been notably absent. More recently, however, when he had been in lodgings during his first year of student life, he had taken cannabis and amphetamines. He had a brief affair, his first, with a coloured girl student, who had 'made a pass at him'. He did not love her and she strongly asserted her love for him. She became pregnant and he and his parents, together with the girl's parents, urged the girl, against her wishes, to have the pregnancy terminated. The girl had made a serious suicidal attempt a few months after the abortion. When he met her subsequently she was quite clearly very angry with him, blamed him for the death of their baby and also stated that she still loved him. It was from this moment that his work began to tail off, at first slowly and then more rapidly.

What became evident was the interplay of two factors: his feeling of guilt for not loving the girl he felt he had exploited, and the remorse over the killing of the first fruits of his biological creativity. Eventually it turned out that the second factor was the more important. He was a remarkably narcissistic young man. The situation was opened up in a face-to-face discussion in brief psychotherapy which consisted of a linking and a working through of both the factors which had been delineated. Therapy produced an entirely satisfactory result. He was able to resume his studies and pass his final examination with distinction. Not all cases, of course, are anything like as easy as this, nor are they as responsive to brief counselling psychotherapy. What one could see from the grid, however, was the absence of early predisposing or other aetiological factors which enabled one to see that the traumatic experience had no really sinister roots and therefore could be dealt with at a fairly superficial level of linking and clarification in therapy. One might ask whether the narcissistic personality was not an adverse pointer. At this stage it did not seem to be although it would have been the point standing out on the grid or schema which would have drawn the therapist's attention to a possibly negative therapeutic component.

Perhaps it has not been stated with sufficient emphasis that adolescence is a normal process involving stresses, risks and abundant opportunities. As in other fields of human endeavour, the greater the conflict between opposing forces, the greater the risk of failure, but the more significant and outstanding the success when it occurs. This applies whether the forces which are contradictory are within the personality of the individual or whether they are outside and working on the subject, i.e. environmentally based. There may also be forces from inside being acted upon by forces outside the individual. Some of the signs of distress which one sees in adolescents are in the course of development and may be looked upon as psychic growing pains. Others show a state of being bogged down so that development seems to be in the doldrums. Nevertheless, spontaneous recovery can and often does take place eventually, and growth is resumed after having been temporarily suspended.

Where there are more severe difficulties, the prognosis may be less favourable but the very openness of the psychic processes during adolescence can be an advantage as far as the efforts of the caring and remedial services are concerned. In contemporary society—which is so different from that which prevailed at the turn of the century, when Victorian materialistic puritanism was still dominant—there are more risks for the adolescent who is not sufficiently integrated and organised to benefit from the freedom and permissiveness. For most adolescents, however, the benefit is great. The period of openness and growth is not curtailed by socially imposed restrictive sanctions. In particular, the capacity to grow into responsible citizenship is no longer thought to be incompatible with enjoying a full life, including especially sexuality. This sexual freedom was stated by Bertrand Russell in his autobiography to be particularly beneficial to students who in former times had such dangerously postponed sexuality.

In life there is much to be said for the Greek concept of balance, and nowhere is the principle so apposite as in the changing world of adolescence.

2

Adolescence and Dropping Out

SHIONA HYATT WILLIAMS

Educational Drop-Outs

Education is one kind of learning experience and the adolescent depends upon a capacity to learn from experience so that he or she can benefit from any educational or academic course. There seem to be two main groups into which educational failure can be divided: (a) those who always underachieve in relationship to their innate capacity; (b) those who drop out or who suddenly fail or who gradually tail off during adolescence at some point in their academic career.

One question to ask is: On whose behalf is the learning experience being undertaken? Sometimes it is on behalf of overambitious, overdriving parents. Sometimes it is on account of demanding, coercive, critical internal parents who may be more or less like the actual parents. Sometimes there is an ambitious teacher or university lecturer or professor who drives his pupils or students on account of *his* ambition, euphemistically labelled his ambition for them.

There are two extremes of adolescents within the dilemma of educational difficulties. At one end there is the son of a labourer or artisan who has done well at school and has the full university grant. Initially, he or she may do very well

25

and then, the nearer it gets to the point of achieving a degree, the more anxiety and/or depression mount and the more failure is likely to take place. This would appear to be due to an inhibition of the ambition to go one better than father or mother. At the other end there is the relatively high frequency of failure of the sons and daughters of academicians, particularly of university teachers. In this case I think the situation is probably more serious because it would indicate the fact that there has been an envious, destructive attack upon the internal parents and upon their success.

Sometimes, educational failure occurs quite early in adolescence—at the grammar school phase or at public school. Sometimes, the failure is due to emotional factors from other areas of life which have been displaced into the educational field. For example, one fourteen-year-old boy did very well indeed at his prep school, in the last year of which his mother died. Suicide of the mother was a possibility but he denied any conscious knowledge of this. When he went on to public school, not very far away from his prep school (so that the displacement was more social than geographical), he began to work less and less effectively. His conscious reason for this was that the teaching methods at his new school were nothing like as good as those of his old school. In point of fact, the teaching methods at his new school were probably a good deal better. What he had done was to displace his distress and failure to mourn for his mother in an adequate way on to the schools so that the school he had 'lost', representing his lost mother, was idealised and the new school was denigrated. It is noteworthy that he got on badly with his new step-mother.

One has to ask a number of questions about any educational failure. What kind of a person is this? Why did he fail when he did? Why did he fail in the way he did? One needs to know something of his past, including the way in which he dealt with stress in his infancy, childhood and in his latency period. Also one needs to know what kind of a feeder he was, as the 'taking-in' is essential in learning. Was he breast fed? Was he bottle fed? What was his weaning like? Were there any difficulties over food and any particular food-fads later on in childhood?

One needs to know something about his distribution of anxiety, whether or not all new demands upon him are occasions for an exacerbation of anxiety. What kind of anxiety is it? Is he dominated more by persecutory anxiety consisting of a feeling of being got-at or threatened, or is he riven by depressive anxiety and overwhelmed by feelings of responsibility, which are all too much for him?

The role of fantasy is important, both conscious fantasy and unconscious. When he is not working, does he think about the work or does he simply work in a routine manner and not take anything away with him and work on it in what would normally be his free time? In the drop-out it is important to understand whether there has been any recent change in the kind of fantasy which predominates and if this something which arose before or after he dropped out.

The role of symbolism is important. What does a particular subject or a particular part of a subject that he is doing or was doing when he became a drop-out stand for? In a medical course, for example, there are occasions when the studies necessarily touch upon something which reminds the student of a very painful, unmetabolised incident in his own life. One woman medical student had lost practically every close member of her family from a variety of gross pathological conditions. She passed all her exams until it came to pathology, which she always failed, in particular if it related to microscopic pathology specimens—a part of a person in fact. As a result of psychotherapy, she was able to understand her unconscious fears, reminiscences, fantasies and even wishes about her own dead relatives, including her mother and father. She passed the pathology examination without difficulty. One young man who was studying law had two years earlier in his student career impregnated a young woman of whom he was not particularly fond; the girl wished to marry him but he was completely unwilling to marry her. Eventually, he persuaded her to have an abortion, after which she reproached him on numerous occasions. At a certain part of his legal studies he found he simply could not work, could

27

not take anything in, and he failed a particular part of his law examinations a number of times. During psychotherapy it emerged that he had been quite unable to mourn the death of what would have been his first-born child. Instead, he had felt harassed and persecuted by this young woman who wanted to marry him and felt resentful that she had almost tricked him into marrying her by becoming pregnant. When his anxieties about terminating life and denials of responsibility had been worked through relatively briefly, this particular young man was able to pass the examination which had for so long held him back.

The role of identification is important. Sometimes young men become very anxious by the close identification with elder or younger siblings, but more particularly with their fathers. Sometimes a young man feels threatened in his sexual identity when there is too close an identification with his mother. For example, one young medical student who had done very well at school went to his mother's old medical school and immediately found himself unable to work. He had been a very good games player and despite quite severe early difficulties at the outset of his medical course the authorities were anxious that he should not drop out altogether. He was given brief therapy which was more of a crisis intervention than anything else and what was apparent was his fear of identification with his mother and the unconscious thought and fantasy that this necessitated his abdication from real manhood. When these situations were sorted out he was able to get over his inability to work, and has since got through his course with no delay at all.

Sometimes there is an identification with an unsuccessful parent so that the very fact of academic success gradually becomes something that the student cannot bear to have for himself, and he then contrives by one means or another to fail and to become a drop-out. It is a matter of loyalty, not only to the external parent but to their intrapsychic images or representations. On the other hand there are those students who are unable to work because of a negative identification with a highly successful parent. Again, not only is there a good deal of envy at the success of the parent

28

and little realisation that that very success had to be worked for, but also a feeling of humiliation and loss of face at the slightest difficulty in the course of study, a difficulty which is followed by an abdication rather than an increased application to study. Some students want and demand instant success and are unwilling to go through the necessary pain and devotion which the achievement of success necessitates. Sometimes the course which they are taking is felt realistically or delusionally by the student to be the parents' course. My mother or my father wanted me to do this, to become a teacher, veterinary surgeon or a dentist and so on.

There are times when a student really is so oppressed by the threat to his own identity and individuality by a course of study which is too closely interwoven with and identified with one or other of his parents that a change may become necessary. Usually such changes themselves are not helpful and are followed by a brief period of relief followed by a further drop-out. There are a few cases, however, where a student who is unsuccessful in one field may change his field of interest and be very successful at that. Sometimes an academic subject may be found to be boring and not suitable to the student. A very brilliant schoolboy may be urged to take an academic course by ambitious schoolmasters and this endeavour may be reinforced by the views of the student's parents. Sometimes a course which ends in disaster in this way may be followed by a completely different course which may be successful. For example, a young man who was reading philosophy at Oxford found that he simply could not read and could not integrate what he had read. But then he was able to get into another less famous university and take agriculture. He had a most successful career, later, introducing constructive changes and innovations in that field. Sometimes the timing of student life is wrong for that particular individual and a few years later the 'drop-out' student has been able to integrate certain other aspects of his life and resume academic activities from a position of greater maturity and subsequently have no further trouble academically. The period of waiting between too early an academic endeavour and too late requires study and consideration.

29

If it is too early the student is not really orientated to the task which is laid before him. If it is too late many other factors including impatience, delay in reaching economic independence, loss of face at being taught by people actually younger than himself and so on can contribute to and complicate the situation.

Subjects taken are important. Sometimes students express their intrapsychic difficulties by choosing a particularly recondite kind of course. The capacity to symbolise is very important. If there is a breakdown in the capacity to symbolise, the subjects taken may include that which should be looked upon symbolically and which instead is taken as 'a thing in itself'. For example, a young woman, a policeman's daughter, decided upon a course in Indo-Pakistani studies. What she was really trying to do was to set the world to rights in an envious identification with her father. The destructive component of her identification with her father finally made itself felt irresistibly and she failed, abdicating from the subject of her choice.

Sometimes the subject matter of the course is overeroticised. For example, a student who became pornographically pre-occupied with the erotic side of art found that he was unable to put his energies into the rest of the course. Interview showed that he had got bogged down in a pornographic, masturbatic relationship to a certain sector of his study. This does not mean that some eroticisation is not usual and in fact normal. It was an old generalisation in a less sexually free day that the medical student's anatomy book always fell open at the full-page picture of the female genitals!

The specificity of dropping out is very important. For example, there may be one particular subject or one particular part of a subject which acts as a block. In that case the symbolic meaning of the subject which is jibbed at and which proves to be a block to development should be investigated. Its elucidation may well help to remove the log-jam and development may then proceed relatively smoothly.

Dropping out, however, may be part of a much larger pattern of breakdown, and in fact in some schizoid patients it may be the first indication that all is not going right.

Sometimes there is a general dropping out of life and at this particular time of adolescence suicidal attempts or dangerous, life-threatening activities are not at all uncommon. Sometimes curious ideologies are sought as escapes from the materialistic needs of the world. The turning to various kinds of religion, strict sects, etc. may be a function of an idealism which is split off from practicality or a function of task avoidance. The capacity to bear tension and states of doubt and uncertainty is very important in academic work and the pursuit of academic qualifications.

Sometimes the dropping out takes place quite late on in the course of study and in that case it is necessary to investigate the meaning of success to the individual. Sometimes it is quite simple: the meaning is to become an adult, with all the implications of adulthood and independence. At other times it means leaving the parents, who may be felt to be unable to do without the physical presence of the adolescent. At other times the adolescent feels he cannot do without one or other of the parents always near him. It is, with college and university students as in school-leavers, the displacement syndrome which sometimes causes late drop-out; in non-apparent drop-outs the overt displacement syndrome is avoided by the individual going on from academic qualification to academic qualification without ever taking on a practical salaried appointment. Often finals are avoided because to pass them is felt to mean an end of something—even of life.

Sometimes dropping out takes place on account of unresolved difficulties in relationship to authority figures, beginning with those of mother and father in the home and usually displaced and reinforced in relationship to teachers, lecturers, professors, heads of department and so on. The more sinister aspect of such attacks on authority figures stem from primal envy in the student, in which the authorities are grudged both their power, knowledge, position, salary, comfort etc. Then, in the clawing down of the authority, the student almost inevitably claws himself down and damages the authority seriously and can damage himself mortally as far as achievement is concerned. These students, should they

31

manage not to become drop-outs, later have great difficulty when they themselves become the authorities. Sometimes they become overauthoritarian and devise hierarchical structures without sufficient delegation or consultation, and sometimes they become unable to differentiate between authoritarianism and the necessary role of leadership. Not all attacks upon authorities and organisations are envious or destructive. Young people may have very legitimate grievances against authorities who either are rather stupid, corrupt or dilatory. The danger is when destructive forces get infused into legitimate communications and endeavours, and the whole issue becomes very much more complicated and confused, often defying solution. The adolescent is likely to become a casualty in such circumstances.

In the crystallisation of individuality there are numerous difficulties in relationship to the self, to the peer group, to authority figures, etc. The role of 'face' (*figura*) is important. Much destructive behaviour in an academic setting is due to the need of both student and authority to avoid losing face. A lot of adolescent rebellion within the nuclear family constellation is due to an inability to climb down and negotiate with parents, and an inability of the parents to climb down and negotiate with the adolescent. Thus, both sides are so intent upon preserving face that they cut themselves off from the possibility of fruitful interaction which might lead to rapprochement and further development within the family setting.

Adolescents are notoriously impatient and are often unable to tolerate dependency, particularly when it is prolonged as it is during an academic course. Incidentally, one of the interesting happenings since the Welfare State became established after the Second World War is the way in which students of working-class parents who are able to get the maximum university grant are really in a far less dependent position in relationship to their parents than students of professional or business parents whose salaries may preclude a student from obtaining a full grant or even from any grant at all apart from the basic £50. I know of a number of students of fairly well-to-do parents who have dropped out because of their intolerance of dependency upon their parents and their resentment of the relative economic independence of their much less economically affluent peers in the academic setting in which they have found themselves.

The whole area is very complicated, but one of the central hinges upon which the issue turns is the way in which the depressive position has been negotiated in infancy and at all other times when it has been necessary or desirable to go through it again. During adolescence there is always a requirement to renegotiate the depressive position. Sometimes this is carried out very much more effectively than in infancy and at other times very much less effectively. A lot depends upon the family supportive network and of course upon the supportive network of the peer group and the academic institution in which the adolescent finds himself. There are a number of distracting factors. Sexuality can be used either in a task-facilitating way or in a task-sabotaging way. Sexuality can be used as a serious distraction so that there is a lack of vital energy left to put into the academic learning process. At other times, as Bertrand Russell said in his autobiography, relatively free sexual relationships of an on-going, but not promiscuous, kind can be task-facilitating as far as educational achievement is concerned. Some other distracting factors consist of an escape into alcohol and drug taking of various kinds, either on an individual or a group basis, and also the turning to pornography in a glib short-circuiting of problems rather than the working through of ambivalent attitudes to sexuality.

The pornographic approach to life as stated by Donald Meltzer consists ultimately of an avoidance of the anxieties and difficulties concerned in the renegotiation of the depressive position. Pornography removes one of the most important components from sexuality and interpersonal relationships, that is the mating and creating within the mind which symbolise the more directly reproductive activities of the body. Thus pornography stultifies the process of sublimation.

The escapes and false gods such as drugs, drink, curious religious sects, escape into purely physical sporting activities,

33

the escape into menial tasks or going to sea, do not invariably end disastrously, but in so far as they represent abdication from the cut and thrust of working through the multitudinous problems of adolescent development, they are likely to have an unfavourable outcome. This does not mean that an unfavourable phase is necessarily permanent, nor does it mean that there are not ways back if after a period of retreat there is a facing of the problems involved and a working through of them. It is at this point that the caring forces can be of maximum use. Let us not be at all nonchalant about the difficulties of growing up. Each generation finds a different world and there is no easy path to paradise, except the time-honoured one of slow and courageous endeavour.

3

Adolescence and Delinquency*

SIMON MEYERSON

> *Luke:*   Let there remain no confusion.
>   The victim ...
> *Monty:* ... and the perpetrator
> *Sam:*   ... have a contract
> *Monty:* ... a collusion
> *Luke:*   Each equally participant
> *Sam:*   Each equally innocent
>
> Extract from the play *The Re-Enactment*

Statistics

Crime statistics reveal links between adolescence and delinquency. In 1967 in Great Britain 50 per cent of all crimes committed were by persons between the ages of ten and twenty-one. In America, 50 per cent of all crimes were committed by persons under eighteen. In both countries—more rapidly and seriously in America—the percentages of crimes committed by the young today show a steady increase with

* I wish to express my indebtedness to the Home Office (particularly Mr Frank Foster OBE, former Director of Borstal After-Care) and to an anonymous trust. Under their initiation and generosity I conducted a lengthy research into adolescent delinquency.

35

clear indications that the onset of serious delinquent activity is starting earlier in modern-day children than was the situation a few years ago. In present-day London, official estimates for the Borough of Camden are that as much as three-quarters of all crimes committed are by children under sixteen.

A conspicuous statistical fact is that age fourteen reveals the highest conviction rate of the total population, with age seventeen a close second. Fortunately, although adolescents are the most frequent offenders they are not the most serious —except for the age-range seventeen to twenty, which has the highest conviction rate for crimes of violence. But, as has been pointed out by adolescent delinquents, 'criminals are those who get caught—the young and the poor'.

The Nature of the Delinquent Act

Basically a delinquent act appears to be an angry defence against love (i.e. hate as a defence against love). Winnicott, in his benevolence, saw a delinquent act as embodying hope. The writer sees it as an expression of despair—failed hope, resulting in a desperate act to establish, by hook or by crook, *a sense of belonging.*

It is perhaps foolhardy to try to oversimplify an explanation for so profound a human communication as a delinquent act. It seems to be a communication about the overwhelming pain experienced in the primary loving where there was a damaging deprivation in being loved *and loving*, thus damaging the sense of belonging. A sense of grievance then damages the development of concern and makes later attempts to achieve a sense of belonging linked with the inflicting of pain or loss.

The word delinquent derives from the Latin *delinquere* which means 'to neglect'. The thesis here is that a delinquent act originates from neglect of the child, who later takes revenge and neglects to care or have concern for others.

A delinquent act appears to be a sadistic, revengeful act. On second glance, it can be seen to be a sadomasochistic act because its perpetration leads to punitive retaliation against the delinquent. So, perhaps, unconsciously and in a naive, doomed way, the delinquent act does embody *hope* of some pairing or contact. Unfortunately, this takes the form of a repeated re-enactment of the early disastrous pairing that originally went wrong between parent and child at the time of failed hope and loss of a sense of belonging. In the re-enactment there is an attempt at reversal of the original roles —now the delinquent is the active doer and the selected victim becomes the recipient of the hurt or loss.

Deep down, the delinquent is an angry, disappointed *idealist*. But his quest to find the idealised figure turns to despair or failed hope because he is unable constructively to forgive the figure who dispossessed him and who did not allow him a loving sense of belonging. Although the delinquent seeks some concrete substitute for the loss or pain, e.g. theft of an article of clothing or violence, the act rarely satisfies fully and is repeated.

Freud pointed out that acting-out was in place of remembering. The delinquent act contains clues about a conflict deriving from the past linking with the present. So an adolescent with anxieties about sexual relations may act-out, say, theft if he felt that in childhood the love had been 'stolen' from him by someone else, even by the withholding mother; or fraud if he felt that he was deceived by his parents' deceptions or inability to really love him or to love him exclusively; or by violence if he felt he was cruelly dealt with or brutally deprived of love, thus battering his sense of belonging.

In some instances a delinquent act can manifest adaptive or normative qualities, e.g. researchers report that in certain subcultures boys who did *not* steal were abnormal. Paradoxically, at times the delinquent act may embody a roundabout attempt at individuality and separate identity, e.g. an adolescent whose parents clung to him symbiotically had to break out of the unhealthy bond. He could not do it himself, committed a delinquent act and a magistrate sent him to Borstal. Sometimes a delinquent act can be the expression of eroticised rage, or a distorted act of intimacy, or even an act of altruism: for example, the adolescent son of a depressed mother who steals from supermarkets partly to give and protect the mother from being overtaxed regarding her giving. A delinquent act may even conceal a poignant attempt at playfulness, especially if the parents had been unable to respond to the child's need for play.

The delinquent act can be a defensive act against unbearable tensions, fears of disintegration, homosexual impulses, depression, murder or suicide. Without the delinquent act as a safety-valve type of defence, the other impulse could have become uncontrollable and acted-out.

Writers on delinquency always focus on deprivation as the central cause of delinquency, but immediately one thinks of some adolescent delinquents, and some notorious criminals, who received endless loving from their mothers. The mothers, by their masochistic martyrdom and excessive loving and capitulating, deprived the future delinquents of the experience of coping with frustration—deprived them of being deprived—so that the child did not develop a sense of belonging but instead developed a false sense of sole ownership, i.e. the world belonging to him.

How does one explain the 'motiveless murders' committed by adolescents in America: as a defence and a violent expression against being 'murdered' by society; as revenge against society failing to provide a sense of belonging; or as an envious attack on anyone who may be believed to have a sense of belonging?

Some Childhood Roots of Delinquency

Since Freud's discoveries, it is generally accepted that delinquency has roots in the perpetrator's infantile history. As many studies of this aspect have already been made, only a few comments will be made here.

If the basic emotional contract between parents and child is good and based on love and an appropriate mutual giving and taking, then the emotional evolution of the relationship is non-delinquent and neither the child nor the parent(s) feel robbed, emotionally 'assaulted', deprived, excluded, exploited or false. If the earlier relationship was good, then at adolescence it is unlikely that delinquent modes will be needed to be acted-out.

Yvonne Blake, the child psychotherapist to whom Winnicott paid tribute in his book *Playing and Reality*, once said jokingly during a seminar that *all* babies are born delinquent. They rob, exploit and attack the breast. They mess, spoil, are inconsiderate and selfish. And it is the 'good-enough' mother (a Winnicottian term) who, by love, helps the baby to forego ruthlessness and become loving.

Gaps or deficiencies leave a 'hunger' for the missing ingredient, and later at adolescence (which is a time of many 'hungers'), the adolescent may steal, or use other baby formulae to try to fill the gap/hunger or inflict it on others. 'Goodenough' fathering is becoming increasingly recognised as a vital factor in the prevention of delinquency, for the mothering relationship depends a great deal on the help and wholeness of *her* relationship with the father. Although she does the mothering, his roles towards her and the child are important. Benign limit-setting, usually inculcated by the mother at the earlier stages, needs a secure definition by the father at later stages.

At all stages in childhood the 'holding' relationship between parents and child—both physical and emotional—should be based on some happy sense of belonging. If based on hate, threat, coercion, double-bind or falseness, the ultimate in holding—imprisonment—may be sought by committing delinquent acts, especially during the bewildering metamorphoses of adolescence. All 'letting-go' stages, such as weaning, or loss of mother to father at Oedipal stage, if not framed within a sense of belonging afforded by parental care and concern, can be experienced by the child as an unforgivable act of robbery and dispossession.

Following in the wake of the repressed Oedipus complex, the 'latency period' (from five until the onset of puberty) is usually characterised as a phase of comparative quiescence and learning and imitation of social values. Nowadays a conspicuous new phenomenon is occurring. Just as many adolescents' problems arise out of the precocious imitation of adults, so the eight- to nine-year-olds are developing a new range of problems that have to do with their needs to be 'imitation adolescents'. This age seems a much neglected area of importance in emotional development, for not only is the child suggestible to socially acceptable modes, but also to anti-social ones picked up, particularly, from older adolescents and from the mass media. A triple-layered phenomenon occurs: the children are mock adolescents, imitating adolescents who are somewhat imitation or mock adults themselves. These pre-pubescents are highly impressionable and are becoming increasingly interested in and influenced by older group trends which are imitated slavishly, whereas adolescents can more easily defy trends as a mode of individuality. At this age a criminal act is frequently seen as adult or adolescent. The power and daring to break the law seems to bring instant status and a special notoriety amongst one's peers. These weeny-boppers, technically outside the law (in England the age of criminal responsibility is ten), are reported as becoming a severe problem.

Adolescence and Delinquency

Adolescence is a time in its own right. Because it is a time of many new experiences, I prefer to call it a time of 'novalescence'. (Novalescence is a term I once found in a book describing a man with qualities that can explore new ideas.)

It is also an anachronistic, Proustian time overlapped by times past—childhood; and it is a projected time, perhaps a premature time, of temptations and obligations overlapping into future time—adulthood.

If times past and present seem filled with real or imagined, remembered or forgotten, times of injustice, adolescence can become preoccupied with putting into effect by a childlike adult way what children are often helpless to achieve—justice. Sometimes this quest for self-made justice leads to one becoming a delinquent.

But even if childhood was experienced as fairly just, the turbulent processes of adolescence can contribute to the adolescent's vulnerability to committing delinquent acts, as the statistics testify.

Broadly speaking, the authorities on delinquency find three main types of adolescent delinquents:

1. Psychopaths—antisocial, affectionless, incapable of feeling guilt.

2. Neurotic delinquents—e.g. 'criminals from a sense of guilt' (Freudian concept).

3. Normal delinquents. At some time or other, all adolescents commit delinquent acts, e.g. to test limits; to prove they are not 'chicken'; to find out how it feels.

The courts, too, in sentencing, usually use these criteria of stereotypes. In actual fact the labelling under the stereotype 'psychopath', for example, while it can condemn the delinquent to ever-increasing doom and cause him to emulate and act-out the label applied, is frequently wrong, as the areas of the personality which *can* experience guilt, remorse and concern are then overlooked and never helped to develop. Also, 'neurotic' delinquents, having guilt and sado-masochistic needs, can frequently trap the authorities into treating them as hardened criminals simply because the crime is repeated. For example, a boy with an adolescent identity problem, afraid of being called a sissy, was committing more and more serious crimes till he got sent to Feltham Borstal. His stated ambition is to go to Portland Borstal (reputed to be the toughest) so that no one can call him 'a nutter or a queer'. He boasts that the maximum security block of Parkhurst Prison is the pinnacle of his ambition— and the State is likely to collude.

In the treatment of delinquents, unless a structure is provided that creates hope of a healthy sense of belonging, statistics will repeatedly reveal not only failure but exacerbation. Prisons do provide a deep and enduring sense of belonging . . . of the criminal kind.

Here follows a brief list of 'pressure points' at adolescence where delinquent acts may manifest themselves as a form of, or in place of, emotional difficulty or breakdown.

Adolescence is a time for sexuality

Generally, it can be said of adolescents that where there is delinquency there will also be a sexual problem. This is hardly surprising as the delinquency usually is a response to some fault in the early loving relationships, causing hostility to be linked to love. Both intimacy and isolation become fused with hostility. The delinquent act can be seen as some ritual involving damaged love. Delinquent acts can become 'sexualised'; for example, the erotic excitement of committing a delinquent act can become conditioned and desired. Sexual acts can become 'delinquentised'; for example, where sex is preferred when 'stolen' from the girlfriend of someone else, or with a girl under sixteen, or, more frequently, 'stolen' from one's own girl by not giving emotionally in return. Sometimes the delinquent act is a defence against guilts about sexuality, and the delinquent act can often be displaced sexual impulses.

Early adolesence is a time of anxious sexuality and some crimes, like compulsive stealing, frequent in early adolescence, do seem to have a masturbatory quality. One is reminded about a fourteen-year-old boy with masturbation anxieties who had a compulsion to steal articulated lorries. Delinquent acts at this age are frequently committed in secrecy by 'loners', but a great deal more seem to be committed by pairs of early adolescents. Friends can share, supporting each other in anxieties, but can also share in acting-out, e.g. hash-smoking, shoplifting, bullying and playing truant. Hetero- and homosexual anxieties can be displaced into a joint delinquent act.

Arson shows a high rate among early adolescents. Psychoanalytic writers often link arson to sadistic masturbatory impulses. A very gentle thirteen-year-old boy was sent to boarding school so that he could 'become a man'. Late one night he got up and set alight a wing of the school. The headmaster did not wish the boy to go to court and psychotherapeutic help was arranged. Pressures to destroy guilts about 'burning desires' to masturbate and about homosexual feelings emerged as factors precipitating his delinquent act.

Adolescent sexuality involves finding a substitute solution to the Oedipal conflict. Excessive Oedipal hurts may leave unresolved rage, revenge and violent jealous feelings. So the emerging sexuality at adolescence releases these and earlier, repressed and partially repressed, hurts—leading to delinquent acts or attacks like theft (to compensate loss of love of mother); or violence (to retaliate against father); or fraud (to get back the lost love or lost object, not by confrontation but by indirect, deceptive means).

It is at the turning point from early- to mid-adolescence, i.e. at the point of beginning movement towards heterosexuality and sexual intercourse, real or fantasised, that delinquent acts are at their highest for both males and females. British statistics show that for any age group of the population the highest number of those convicted were aged fourteen. There is greater social and intrapsychic conflict in having to face the emotional tasks of achieving a sense of belonging through heterosexual relations.

The delinquent act may conceal a pathetic need for contact, a desperate need to achieve a sense of belonging at almost any price. Take the much-publicised phenomenon of the 'gang-bang': while seeming tough and daring, it hides the sexual inadequacies of the members and may have more to do with shared homosexual anxieties than with a heterosexual act; the gang-bang unites the males homosexually under the guise of heterosexual proof and unity.

Adolescence is a time of increased aggressive impulses

In addition to sexuality, the adolescent can become overwhelmed by an influx of aggressive feelings and impulses, physical growth and the need for physical action. A delinquent act can consist of a powerful combination of sexuality and aggression, e.g. the excitement and aggression that is involved say in house-breaking, dangerous driving or other delinquent acts in which overt violence is a feature. But in *all* delinquent acts hostility is a feature—and when hostility is fused with aggression, violence can easily be an end result.

Aggression, in some degree, is a normal accompaniment of

43

adolescence and physical growth. Normal adolescents can feel aggressive but mostly sublimate it into sport, but because adolescence is also a time for rebellion, those who harbour a grievance from earlier relationships can now openly include exaggerated retaliatory aggression in relationships with parents, peers, authority figures and others.

With the resuscitation of old Oedipal struggles at adolescence, the physical 'triumph' of violence and aggression is possible, as is brought home in fights where adolescents brutally beat up fathers, teachers and other adults because of actual physical superiority. Jack was an extremely aggressive adolescent whose presence set up the tension of exuded violence and he was much feared in the neighbourhood. As a child he frequently had to get out of the family's only bedroom so that his mother, who was a prostitute, could 'do business'. As an adolescent he achieved great notoriety for beating up males, especially in the presence of their female friends. He himself had the sexiest girl of his gang and her attractiveness made her admired by males, who would then get beaten up for 'staring'. Jack, secretly, was in fact sexually impotent and feared being called 'queer'. His earlier feelings had made him violently jealous so that he felt confused between sexuality and violence.

Violence can be expressed outside the family by a gravitation to gangs for anti-parental and anti-authority purposes where the main ethos is to punish, castrate, denigrate, destroy, spoil, e.g. the Spoilers or Hell's Angels where violence is strength and conscience is weakness. It is interesting to note that some adolescents can be angels at home and absolute 'devils' when with their gang.

Of course there is healthy aggression. The adolescent has to prepare for manhood. Struggles involve feelings of dominance/submission, active/passive, adult/child, male/female, strong/weak and penetration desires. When exaggerated aggression is a manifestation of disturbance, especially paranoid fears of authority or of homosexuality, it can trigger easily and quickly into violence. Adolescent delinquents can graduate from theft to assaults. Theft persists but can have added dimensions, e.g. house-breaking and theft, robbery with violence, muggings, assaults with more violent components like knifing. Where in early adolescence 'conning' homosexuals for money might suffice, in later adolescence 'queer bashing' is in evidence. Gangs too can build their hierarchies according to capacity for violence or strength. Violence usually seems to be derived from the need to discharge 'unjust' pain which the adolescent experienced in childhood but also from the pains of adolescence itself which need to be discharged, e.g. by bullying. If the pain experienced in the past was particularly brutal, brutalisation can now set into the pattern of relationships.

As mentioned, crimes of violence statistically reveal the highest frequency in the seventeen- to twenty-year-old group of the population. Late adolescence is a powerful and irreversible turning point. There is the reality of social pressures such as careers, education, wage earning, responsibility for others and self both emotionally and legally. Inability to cope can lead to failure, dropping out or a subculture membership where violence is a prerequisite for survival. On the threshold of adulthood physical strength emerges into prominence and if other social requisites are not complied with, physical strength or force also seem 'natural' as formulae for coping with the increased internal (emotional and physical) pains as well as uncertainties in the external (social) world.

Frustration escalates during this phase of disturbed adolescence; there is a more 'rapistic' type of 'getting'—robbery, mugging, taking and driving away, housebreaking. But, in the neurotic type of late adolescent, the isolated violent act can be a defence against suicide, disintegration, identity vacuum—a cry for help, sadomasochistic and guilt-ridden as it may be.

If one tries to analyse violence, one becomes increasingly aware that it is a compulsive reaction to hurt by being excluded from a sense of belonging. Gang members can feel, at the height of gang violence, an almost orgasmic sense of belonging. All personal differences are forgotten and a sense of belonging holds sway when the violence of a gang is focused on an outside target. Daubings all over the south

London district of the Elephant and Castle advertised 'Aggro Sunday Night Tally Ho', which was a north London gang's meeting place. Truck loads of delinquents armed with chains, knives, knuckle-dusters and hammers were expected in gangs of tightly-knit allegiance, but on this occasion fortunately no gang violence took place as, during the week, someone had daubed all over north London 'Aggro Sunday Night Mile End'—a tough district in east London.

If one looks at the most violent adolescents in the world, whether it be Hell's Angels, Arab terrorists, Northern Irish adolescents or Blacks in American ghettoes, one sees that the causes are to do with dispossession and deep hurt to their early sense of belonging. Their act of violence—beneath the destruction—involves, and gives, an altruistic sense of belonging—momentary and complicated as it may seem.

Adolescence is a time of identity confusion

When working with adolescent delinquents, one is struck by the fact that somehow or other when the adolescent is confused, frightened or anxious, the perpetration of a delinquent act creates a structure which momentarily may give the adolescent some feeling of identity.

Adolescence brings with it the ambiguities and ambivalences of identity confusion. This confusion creates tension; cross-wires which emotionally healthy adolescents can slowly unravel and work through. But adolescents can feel persecuted by these feelings and instantly try to discharge the doubts. For example, if an adolescent is in doubt about his masculinity or cannot cope with depression or even anger, he may bully a weaker boy and leave this victim feeling a 'sissy', depressed and angry. This method, involving the need for instant projection and an instant 'receptacle', instead of using inner emotional means to resolve the confusions, is a frequent cause of delinquent acts at adolescence.

Early- and mid-adolescence are times of identity struggle, particularly regarding peer group modes of acceptance. Many delinquent acts at this stage have a 'proving' motive, especially to prove sexual or tough identity. This is usually done by acts of daring. Violence is the simplest 'proving' offence if the adolescent is physically strong: if not, other acts become necessary. For instance, drinking and drug offences by adolescents between the ages of fourteen and sixteen years have drastically increased. The drugs may grant momentary relief from identity pain and confusion, but in addition to the drug offence, the potential for other offences can become unleashed.

If identity confusion has not been fairly well resolved by late adolescence, which should be a time for evolving a sense of direction, certainty, self-sufficiency and a harmony between feeling and action, then identity may need to be forcibly and despairingly established—concretely—e.g. by violence to prove manliness, especially if brutality and deprivation robbed the child of a sense of belonging in his early years. At late adolescence there are higher rates of breakdown, suicide and depression in neurotics, but more numerous and more serious delinquent acts in the 'affectionless', e.g. use of weapons that can kill—knives, hammers and guns. Nowadays, with the modern myth-making television concept of 'the criminal as hero', even the identity of the criminal seems to feel more acceptable to the late adolescent than isolated, fragmented, depersonalised insignificance.

What has become evident over the last few years is the movement away from the 'usual crimes of early adolescence' to an imitation of crimes performed by older age groups, that is 'stolen identity' crimes. Resort to frauds particularly at late adolescence, where identity crises cannot be overcome, are becoming noticeable. A cheque fraud involves not only a theft of money belonging to another but also a theft of an identity. Bisexual identity conflicts are not unusual in those who resort to fraud.

Adolescence is a time for losses and a time for gains

The high speed of losses (e.g. of infantile dependent bonds) and gains (e.g. sexuality, social activities, territories, intellectual, physical and emotional strength) can lead to delinquent acts to recoup losses or to exploit or mismanage gains.

47

With age fourteen showing the highest conviction rate in both sexes of the total population, the possibility of loss of the infantile self as a cause in the sharp incidence of theft seems likely. With the loss of the infantile self there is a concomitant loss of the former parental supports. But there are also too many gains to cope with, so there is usually a rush to peer group support with the need for triumph and contempt and repudiation of the parents.

If the losses take place too rapidly, the pressure to exploit the gains in the cause of retaliation appears greater, e.g. sudden rebellion against parents, followed by sudden acts of theft and violence or promiscuity to prove how 'adult and independent' one is. It seems that when losses and gains occur too rapidly for the ego to master the situation, the possibility of impulsive delinquent acts is high. If neither the parents nor the child find 'a good distancing' or 'timing' for empathetic separation, this loss-gain imbalance can lead to disturbing feelings that may compulsively need to be acted-out in a desperate attempt to contradict these feelings, to impulsively 'grab' transition-objects for support. Where parents are too far distant, emotionally out of appropriate contact with the early adolescent, or vice versa, or where the parties want to perpetuate old infantile ties and cling to bonds incestuously or childishly tinged, the adolescent may resort to some desperate measure, like getting caught for a delinquent act, so that an outside agency can be brought in to effect a separation. Outside agencies, unfortunately, can sometimes try to remake the anxiety-causing bond rather than help the adolescent and the parents to make an appropriate shift in relationships. Sometimes a delinquent act is perpetrated so that the adolescent gets the court to order the parents to keep care of him. This way the adolescent manipulates a perpetration of infantile bonds which he fears severing.

Adolescence involves a 'time-splash' of lingering past influences, pressing present desires and the immediate prospect of 'future' gratifications. In fact, as has been said, adolescence is delicately poised upon the overlapping tensions of childhood past, adolescent present, and adult future. Some parents shudder at the prospect of their fourteen-year-old with childish mind and adolescent emotions and an adult body. They see these as almost perfect ingredients for a thoughtless, impulsive, irresponsible act if the adolescent is subjected to temptation.

Adolescence is a time for fluctuation

Many delinquent acts are perpetrated in the highs and lows of moods, e.g. when emotional impulses are overexciting or when depression is too great and needs to be relieved. Because adolescence is a time of hyperactivity and hyperimpulsiveness, it can be expected that the projection and acting-out will be great, thus increasing the risk of delinquent expression.

In short, Adolescence Is a Time For Establishing New Ways of Belonging

Adolescence is a time for many things. It is a 'volatile time of risk and opportunity' (Hyatt Williams); transition and transgression; impulsiveness and instant gratification; projection rather than containment; acting-out rather than holding-in; impatience rather than self-denial. It is a time for a mixture of diverse, opposite and extreme feelings and counter-feelings—encroachment and counter-encroachment: a twilight land of childhood clinging and adult groping; 'weanings', confusions, instabilities, uncertainties; responsibility and irresponsbility; of finding out and blinding out. It is a time of testing the me and you of identity; me, not-me, mine, not-mine; possible, not-possible; infatuations; situations, complications; the outer limits, the inner limitlessness; authority and extremity—the action, the reaction, the counteraction. It is a time for love and hate, for sadness and excitement for sex and violence; for loneliness and for gangs; for compliance and defiance; for expression, sublimation and repression; for self-discovery and self-denial; for change and refusal to change; and for destruction. In fact, it

49

affords an endless repertoire for belonging, for creativity, and for finding one's own special mode of interpersonal being.

At adolescence, new and special modes of belonging crystallise. The family as one's central base to sustain a sense of belonging, as in childhood, undergoes profound change. Now a sense of belonging is to be found beyond the family in social ties that require perhaps different criteria for membership, acceptance and identity.

Social and interpersonal relationships crystallise demandingly in adolescence, requiring a foregoing of childhood 'privileges' and also requiring extra-familial ties and responsibilities that can, in immature adolescence, be too exacting and overburdening. So some adolescents can be tempted to move into relationships split-off from ordinary reciprocity and find ties that can give vent to stored-up hostility, defiance and anti-social obligation.

As with sexuality, the *pairs* are important in delinquency. Corrupt pairing leads to reinforcement of perverse or corrupt existing bonds. Healthy pairing is crucial both in preventing delinquent acts and in treatment: if no good pairing occurs after release from Borstal, within three months a delinquent act will in nearly all cases be repeated. For example, a delinquent was released from Borstal to a hostel and within four hours was arrested for car theft because, on his arriving at the hostel the warden neglected to pair with him in some accepting way to give him a sense of belonging. Another delinquent paired with him and out of their 'togetherness' they decided to steal a car for a joy-ride.

It should be pointed out that the familial sense of belonging will influence the adolescent's extra-familial mode of finding a new sense of belonging. If there is not a 'goodenough family', the family can be its own criminal subculture. For example, there can be conscious or unconscious parental complicity, corruption and inconsistent morality: 'I told you not to steal.' 'You said I can steal from Jews.' 'But he isn't a Jew. He's a Protestant.' 'But Dad steals from his boss, who is a Protestant.' 'Yes, dear, but he's a rich Protestant.' In the absence of a goodenough environment, emotional and social factors conspire for dangerous gangs to thrive. The primary aim of subculture membership is to get some form of identity, some form of discharge of anxiety, sexuality and aggression and to underly defiance and rebellion in such a way as to have recognition, support and reassurance which has become difficult to get in the wider 'authority-ridden, complying society'—even though gangs can demand greater conformity than the culture at large. The gang arises out of disillusionment about a sense of belonging as fostered by parental, authority figures and the society, as well as arising from a need to act-out in a structure that does not exaggerate social criteria that induce feelings of failure or rejection. The oversimplified formula of screwing (stealing), screwing (sex) and screwing (fighting) to cope with complex society (as well as with disturbed self identities) can underly the gang's revengeful self-made sense of belonging.

The *loner* cannot pair because of past deep hurt, distrust and an almost total despair about achieving a sense of belonging with others. His delinquent act can be perpetrated as an angry grievance or protest, e.g. the murder of a lonely old woman. Nevertheless, there is, sadly, a pairing with the victim, momentary as it may be, or with the punishing authorities, i.e. being looked after even though in a sado-masochistic pairing.

The neglected, unwanted, dispossessed can, by a delinquent short-cut, change from feeling totally unwanted to being 'the most wanted man in the country'.

A Brief Note on Female Delinquents

It is a well-known saying that 'bad boys resort to crime and bad girls to sex'. Today this no longer is as true as it was.

Statistics usually show high breaking-and-entering or violence for boys while for girls there are not usually the 'penetrative masculine' delinquent acts. Girls might play truant, shoplift, take drugs or become prostitutes, receive proceeds of male crime, or become pregnant 'illegitimately' (receptive delinquent acts).

51

The female conviction rate is minimal compared with that of males. Girls appear to cope with early parental loss of love by getting into dependent relationships, resorting to promiscuity or prostitution to achieve a sense of belonging (more easily done by females). But there is increasing evidence—although the statistics have to be kept in perspective —that the trend in adolescent female delinquency is changing to a marked degree. In 1967 some 2,000 girls in Britain were convicted of shoplifting but violent crimes were minimal. In 1970 nearly 2,000 girls were convicted of crimes involving violence. For example, recently a fourteen-year-old girl, caught shoplifting, attacked the policewoman, knocked her to the ground and started hammering her head on the pavement. Gangs of adolescent girl muggers have been reported roaming London streets at night. Female delinquency is not only on the increase but their delinquent acts are beginning to reveal patterns which previously were thought possible only for male delinquents, e.g. a female teeny-bopper was arrested for carrying a hammer which was used to break into a back entrance of an hotel where the Osmond Brothers were staying. The use of the hammer is sometimes found in late adolescent male gang violence of a very disturbed and serious kind.

With cultural changes, dual morality changes and with the growth of consciousness raised by Women's Lib, there does appear to be a greater element of masculine identity in female delinquents. In any event, in the past a great majority of female delinquents frequently presented strong masculine traits in their disturbed identities.

Besides the usual causes such as deprivation and a disturbed mother-child relationship, a factor that has been neglected is the girl's disturbed relationship with the father. Either he is absent and the girl compensates by becoming male or has a need to attack him; or he is present but brutal, ineffectual or seductive. This leads to a devaluation of her femininity.

Some psychiatrists see 'Unisex' as being a focal reason for these newly-developed female delinquent traits. Others see the cause as linked to the affluent society, e.g. parents,

especially mothers, too busy earning money or working to
provide against material deprivation, are actually causing
secondary maternal deprivation.

The Observer recently quoted a psychiatrist:

'Twenty years ago a working-class girl was type-cast. She
washed the dishes, left school as soon as possible, helped
mum and was in by ten o'clock. Now her horizons have
been widened. She's no longer happy with her lot in the
shop or factory waiting to get married. She mixes with
boys on equal terms. She doesn't sit at home as the passive
receiver of stolen goods: she may well go along on the
house-breaking job herself and then perhaps line up
another girl to do a job without the boys.'

Broadly speaking, it may be said that many females, not
only delinquents, are today becoming increasingly involved
in the emotional 'crime' of theft of the male identity. But
perhaps they are revolutionaries unconsciously heralding
and acting-out cultural change by *reclaiming* from males
that part of a sense of belonging which belongs to females
too.

4

Acting-out, Rebellion and Violence

ARTURO VARCHEVKER and
BRIAN MUIR

> Turning and turning in the widening gyre
> The falcon cannot hear the falconer;
> Things fall apart; the centre cannot hold;
> Mere anarchy is loosed upon the world,
> The blood-dimmed tide is loosed,
> And everywhere the ceremony of innocence is drowned;
> The best lack all conviction,
> While the worst are full of passionate intensity.
>
> (W. B. Yeats, 'The Second Coming')

Introduction

The word 'adolescence' comes from the Latin and means 'to blossom, to grow'. The authors believe that, to a degree, acting-out, rebellion or violence are part of normal adolescent growth and development. But at times these phenomena may merge into actions which are intolerable and overwhelming, not only to those persons linked to the adolescent or to society but to the adolescent himself.

Adolescents are part of the society in which they live.

54

They belong to families, groups and institutions. Adolescents may stay out late or smoke hash or mug a victim or be drafted to kill another human being in Vietnam. Their behaviour will be the expression, whether conscious or unconscious, of the emotions, frustrations and impulses going on inside themselves as well as in aspects of society that influence them. Only when this type of overall understandis used is it possible to assess meaningfully when acting-out, rebelliousness and violence constitute a dangerous and disturbed type of behaviour as compared with the more 'normal' process of growing in adolescence.

Acting-Out

The concept of acting-out has its origins in psychoanalysis. However, nowadays this term is more widely and loosely used. It is used to describe the more dangerous forms of antisocial behaviour, where the impulse may lead to burglary, physical attacks or even homicide. It also describes other situations where there is little or no damage involved. For example, the adolescent girl who, because she did not like the handbag which her mother had bought for her, forgets it and leaves it on the bus, or the adolescent boy who will fill himself with 'booze' before a party, because he is nervous about seeing a girl there on whom he had a 'crush'. In this way he 'acts-out' his feelings of insecurity.

The first reference to the term 'acting-out' appeared in 1905 in Freud's postscript to the Dora case,[1] where he writes: "because of the unknown quantity in me which reminded Dora of Herr K [an important person in the patient's life] she took her revenge on me as she wanted to take her revenge on him, and deserted me as she believed herself to have been deceived and deserted by him. Thus, she *acted-out* an essential part of her recollections and phantasies instead of reproducing them in the treatment'. In this, action replaces memory. Freud saw acting-out as a re-enactment of some early traumatic event or situation, partly disguised and usually distorted towards a wish-fulfilment,

55

and as an attempt to change the past and to master the original anxiety.

Acting-out in adolescence has been described by Anna Freud[2] as 'age-adequate'. At this stage she says 'recall of the past is at a minimum and reliving of past experiences at its height'.

Rycroft[3] in his *A Critical Dictionary of Psycho-Analysis* says of acting-out:

'A patient is said to be acting-out if he engages in activity which can be interpreted as a substitute for remembering past events. The essence of the concept is the replacement of thought by action and it implies that either (a) the IMPULSE being acted-out has never acquired verbal representation, or (b) the impulse is too intense to be dischargeable in words, or (c) that the patient lacks the capacity for INHIBITION. . . .'

Acting-out is closely associated with the phenomenon of transference—another term deriving from psychoanalysis which is now in more general use. Transference is a process by which a person, without being aware of it, displaces on to others feelings and phantasies he has for other figures in his life, especially those of his early childhood.

Acting-out as a communication in adolescence

The authors conclude that some acting-out is necessary for growth, but this is especially pertinent in adolescence where it is a universally pervasive phenomenon. It is seen as a communication. And even though it carries an impulsive quality that contrasts with the most integrated aspects of the individual, beneath the exaggerated communication there is a defence against catastrophic anxieties, a cry for help and at the same time an indication of hope. Adolescence is a time of rapid changes and fluctuations in emotional states which are often expressed in actions rather than in words. At puberty reproduction becomes a real possibility and physical strength and growth accelerates. The adolescents is now coming closer to the world of adults. He feels quite strongly that he has to quickly find new solutions to new problems.

The adolescent's available means of communication are not always sufficient to rise above and contain and modify his impulses and phantasies by some integration with adequate reality testing.

He has a marked tendency to see others in terms of their status (age, role) in a hierarchy, rather than as individuals with their own needs and feelings. This status-orientated view leads him to expect to be regarded by others in a like fashion, and not as an individual with needs and anxieties of his own. It is likely that this tendency is encouraged by our own adult attitude and is influenced by the culture of the group or society. One frequently finds the relationship between a youngster and his father to be of a very rigid kind based on a pattern of what they imagine their different roles to be. Neither of them can feel at ease in bringing into the relationship more personal feelings which might threaten their overt social identity or role. In this way the relationship becomes impoverished. But the suppressed feelings can be transferred into another person or situation. A tendency develops to deny or split-off those feelings which are imagined to be unacceptable and to locate them in someone else. At times such feelings or conflicts may be 'acted-out' in situations different from those of their origin. For example, the adolescent who has stolen a car perhaps acts out his frustration and resentment at being infantilised by his parents.

By transferring all the problems on to others, sometimes he may create a situation in which he cuts off the possibility of help from outside. Parents, teachers, therapists, friends or society, under these circumstances, do not have anything worthwhile to offer in his eyes. If pressure is brought to bear on him, either from without or within, this could lead to violent, rebellious acting-out. The anxiety that has been stirred up by this pressure is so strong, that it is as if the adolescent's whole being is threatened.

The fact that adolescents are much more liable to express their phantasies in action and motility, rather than in words,

57

leads some people (including parents and psychiatrists) to righteously shrug off further attempts at communication. This attitude can exacerbate deeper attempts at acting-out unless parents, teachers, psychiatrists etc, who relate to adolescents, can make full use of, and understand and respect, bodily communications, gestures and actions—at times even violent ones. These acted-out expressions are communications of important adolescent frustrations, confusions and anxieties.

A seventeen-year-old boy with a history of having been brutally punished by his father, was referred to a residential institution because of delinquent behaviour. For many weeks he had remained a peripheral member of the group. He was in a permanent state of irritation and distrusted everybody, especially the staff. Suddenly, following a football match, in which staff also participated, he exhibited a striking change of attitude towards his group and his treatment. During the game he displayed a great deal of verbal and physical aggression, especially towards the staff. After the game, when he realised he would not be punished he began to feel sorry and express regret for his roughness. His hostility and the communication of it, were accepted. In the game he channelled his violent feelings towards the people who reminded him of his father. The residential setting provided for him a safer and less persecuting situation, which enabled a shift in his attitude. A subsequent easing of verbal communication and a less rigid status-orientated view started to develop.

Management of acting-out

Workers with adolescents will hopefully be able to find within themselves the virtuosity and creativity to evolve a technique by which the understanding and handling of adolescent acting-out can be enhanced. The intensity and frequency of the acting-out should determine the attitude towards the adolescent. Re-inforcement of boundaries and limits, prohibition and treatment are resources available, but we hope that through this exploration of acting-out in adolescence we have contributed to a growing understanding of it that will facilitate the growth of trust and the enrichment of relationships with adolescents.

Winnicott has stated in 1968,[4] 'immaturity is important and healthy for adolescents. In it is contained the most exciting features of creative thought, new and fresh feelings, ideas for new living.' And he goes on to say that 'adults must not abdicate otherwise the adolescent becomes prematurely, and by false process, adult . . . confrontation may need to replace understanding at times' and 'confrontation belongs to containment that is non-retaliatory, without vindictiveness, but having its own strength'. We believe that it is always important to share with the adolescent the reason for doing what you do, for the stand you are taking. Authority must be assumed but without being authoritarian and arbitrary particularly in areas of responsibility and dependency.

Aspects of Rebellion

Main[5] describes adolescence as the period of life in which disillusionment and reality testing are at their height, and so at times life can be experienced by the adolescent as painful and horrifying. The idealised, perfect parents he has held through his childhood are suddenly being questioned and scrutinised. They become the parents who could be mistaken, who are not as understanding as he would like them to be. There is also the realisation that one day his parents will grow older and die giving way to him as an adult. There is so much that the adolescent has to cope with that at times he may overwhelmed by it.

In adolescence there is a need for appropriate identification models partly as a reassurance that aggressive impulses can be contained and limited, without retaliation and vindictive or punitive reprisal that can escalate into violence or uncontrollable hate and anger. There is also a need for identification models to push against, that is, to rebel healthily against. Such a process is necessary for the establishment

59

of autonomy and the sense of integrity—being a real person in one's own right.

More disturbed adolescents experience a feeling of having an identity imposed upon them by their parents or other outside authority figures. Their rebellion is usually seen as negative. They attempt to refute their identity. At the same time they often seem to provoke from the parents the very sort of imposition they fear, as though they felt that there were no other way of maintaining any sense of value in the parents' eyes, and for fear of losing the parents they depend upon and need. Thus rebellion can take the form of doing the opposite of what the parents want, for example, failing at school or dropping out of university. Such rebellion is self-destructive. Its aim is to achieve a feeling of independence but the independence is spurious, and in fact the dependent bond with the parents is actually reinforced. This type of rebellion is often rationalised by the adolescent as an attempt to live up to his ideals and to renounce the values of what he considers to be a hypocritical and corrupt society.

Authority figures—parents, teachers and others who work with adolescents—who have themselves failed to resolve their own adolescent rebellious problems and identity crises are often liable to reduce such problems in adolescents but to unconsciously collude in promoting a deficient aggressive way of relating.[6]

In neurotic adolescents the rebellion tends to take the form of a chronically irritating and provocative relationship where the parents, etc. are driven to despair by the feeling that nothing they say or do for the adolescent is right, while the adolescent sees the parents, etc. as unsatisfactory, feeble, old-fashioned, harsh or degraded figures of whom he is ashamed. There are constant rows and fights, usually Oedipally coloured. Despite this, the adolescent is caught up in a dependent relationship in which he, at times, feels helplessly passive and from which he may despair of ever growing free.

In the normal adolescent, rebellion is more effective and healthy, in that it is directed towards achieving an emancipation from the parents, a loosening of incestuous Oedipal ties and, therefore adaptive. Other figures are sought: peer group or parental substitutes like teachers, who are seen as better than the parents or more understanding. These are frequently distorted perceptions, but they serve to assist the adolescent in severing his ties. Much of the negativism and defiance seen in these young people are expressions of the need to push against the parents—a process of boundary discovery for the ego.

In the sick adolescent the rebellion does not always achieve or serve a more constructive purpose, i.e. a defence against anxieties of being invaded and overwhelmed by possessive and controlling parents who see the child as an extension of themselves rather than as a person in his own right. Rather, the opposite. Their rebellion deepens their negative bonds; they experience themselves then as selfless and dependent infants who have to control and manipulate needed and hated parental figures. Complying is seen as an overwhelming, smothering trap. Violent rebellion becomes a defence against such helplessness. These modes of defence are often incorporated into the character structure and continue into adulthood.

In all adolescents there are frequently problems involving sexual identity, an area in which he or she is struggling to achieve a sense of masculinity or femininity and a sense of emotional and physical ego. Thus, at times, acting-out, whether it be rebellious or violent (within acceptable limits of tolerance in quantity and intensity), may well be a contributory part or a necessary step in a process of accommodating and integrating new experiences into the personality. In all adolescent rebellion, whether normal, neurotic, borderline or delinquent, there is an inherent conflict between dependency and emancipation.

Violence

Violent behaviour in adolescents is traditionally linked with a diagnosis of delinquency or psychopathy, but in fact, although it is a predominant phenomenon in this category of disturbed adolescent, it is seen from time to time in neurotic, psychotic and in normal adolescents. However, when repetitive and severe it indicates particularly severe anxieties and a fragile ego.

It is generally agreed that repeated acts of violence in adolescents are found to be associated with great emotional pressures, seemingly inexpressible in any other way, and resulting from unmodified infantile drives which have never been properly tamed or sublimated by satisfactory and consistent early relationships. In other words, violence is commonly regarded as the result of some sort of deprivation. The violent adolescent feels he has been cheated of something and is owed something. Violence in adolescence is also seen as a defence against passive or homosexual strivings. This is particularly true in boys. It represents an attack on authority (i.e. the weak, degraded, absent peripheral or failed father), or attempts to deny the passive strivings which defend against Oedipal incestuous wishes towards the mother, and simultaneously provides a covert (and sometimes more overt) homosexual gratification by association with a gang or peer group devoted to violence and destruction. Promiscuity in girls can be seen to serve a similar function. In boys sadism and cruelty are felt to be preferable to the fear and ignominity of passive strivings, 'queerness' and being seen as effeminate. Such anxieties are usually behind the episodes of 'queer bashing' indulged in sometimes by gangs of youths, and which occasionally end tragically in murder.

Antisocial violent acts can also be seen as symptoms of guilt feelings. Such actions are more likely to lead to adult rejection and hostility than any other. These increase the child's feelings of personal worthlessness and guilt. In other words, as often as not these forms of acting-out make the child's worst fears come true. The youngster must perpetrate these violent acts in order to make his guilt feelings tangible. At the same time he subjects his parents (or the caring authority) to a test as to whether, despite his aggressive impulses, he is acceptable to them and valued by them.

If we go into the history of violent adolescents we find that the earliest phase of trust and confidence in the consistence and reliability of a 'goodenough' mother has never existed reliably. Instead, early in life, a manipulative, controlling, sadomasochistic bond developed between mother and child. There is usually a history of a battle of wills, a battle for power and an absence of any reliable dependable relationship, which is the prerequisite for the development of a stable self and a sense of being valued and wanted and accepted intrinsically for one's own sake.

Omnipotence is maintained and the adolescent dare not relinquish it because he feels that if he does, he will lose everything and either be rejected totally, or annihilated leaving his real self in total chaos, exposed and vulnerable, in a hostile world full of dangerous persecutory and unreliable objects. He must therefore, in an effort to deny his overwhelming dependency needs and feelings of helplessness, constantly prove to himself that the environment has no power over him.

The child feels that it cannot trust the mother and if he did the only possible result would be total aloneness, disintegration, madness and total annihilation of self. This is why the phenomenon of action is a central one in violent delinquent behaviour. No internal conflict is felt. It is prevented by creating a conflict with the outside world, i.e. the pain must be externalised.

Thus a central issue in the treatment of violent adolescents is by a slow build up of a trusting relationship to help them to grow the strength to internalise their conflicts—a terribly painful process with inevitable depression. At the same time, the adolescent needs help to relinquish his sadistic omnipotent view of himself and his situation and to improve his reality testing. He has to give up his magical thinking, learn to have the courage to be more in touch with and control his own vulnerable feelings which cause violence. Thereby he will hopefully acquire an ability to appreciate himself as a person of value in his own right. It is only then that he will be able to identify with others as people in their own right, with feelings and anxieties like his own.

A word should be said about privacy. Adolescents need privacy—emotional as well as spacial. When there is no provision for this, no 'personal territory', e.g. a bedroom or cubicle with lock, for personal possessions, violence is much more likely to occur. The 'territorial imperative' and the instinct for personal acquisitions and property are powerful motives in human behaviour. Too often we see examples of institutions where deprived children are further dehumanised and depersonalised by being denied privacy, personal possessions and clothing and hence robbed of their identity.

Management involves guardianship, caring and continuity. The interrelationship and relative proportions of these three factors need to be balanced flexibly. Continuity is more important in the case of more deprived adolescents in institutional settings where any interruptions and discontinuity will evoke feelings of loss with massive anxieties that can lead the adolescent to behave as though he has been violently and unjustly robbed.

Most people find outbursts of apparently irrational violent behaviour as the most puzzling, frightening, painful and infuriating of human actions. When an episode of disruptive or violent behaviour occurs in an adolescent, it is important to understand why. If we accept that any acting-out is a primitive sort of communication arising from intense anxieties, we must ask what it means. What has been missed, what has not been understood, what has been going on in the adolescent that we have failed to see or comprehend?

Under conditions of severe stress, violence can occur in the most integrated individual. But, by and large, adolescents who exhibit recurrent violent behaviour are relatively unintegrated individuals with poor capacity to contain their own anxieties and impulses. They have a weak ego structure because of serious parental failure and violence can be precipitated by relatively minimal stress. It is therefore important to stress that a healthy *milieu* is one which affords a free and open communication system in order that anxieties and feelings may be freely voiced and shared. This open interpersonal climate assists in containing and verbalising disruptive anxieties and effects.

The aim and essence of management is prevention but

simultaneously there should be a fostering of more healthy ego growth. However, prevention is not always possible. Many disturbed adolescents are isolated and resist any attempt to engage with them. Furthermore, unresolved, unconscious, ambivalent and violent phantasies and conflicts in staff members, parents, or other caring persons, are frequently activated by adolescents who then respond by acting-out. It is important to bear these projection systems in mind, as they need to be taken into consideration at all times.

When an outburst of violent behaviour does occur, the adolescent concerned is the victim of overwhelming panic and disruptive rage, which further fragments an already poorly integrated ego. One can frequently see this lack of integration and fragmentation of the personality manifesting in a more subdued way as disruptiveness in the classroom or in any other organised activity situation whether work or play. There is an aimlessness and lack of purpose, which has a destructive quality, an inability to concentrate and focus on any task or group activity. It is of no avail to appeal to the 'better nature' of these adolescents, because they lack the capacity for concern or to feel guilt or remorse. In the long-term caring situation the aim should be to foster growth of these qualities.

When an attack of violence does occur the adolescent needs firm holding both physically and psychologically—by persons who do not hate him. This may not be easy with a strong and almost fully grown young person. But, they should never be left alone with their panic. They need non-retaliatory containment with an attempt to understand. It should not be forgotten that those in charge have limits to their capacities, and sometimes will meet with failure. Then the young person will have to be removed and secured in a safe place where he is not a danger to himself or to others.

Violence and Acting-Out as a Defence against Depression

If a youngster has to rebel in a violent manner which may be destructive to himself or other people or property, we may assume that something has gone radically wrong with rela-

65

E

tionships with parents and other authority figures. He is in other words struggling against such resented identifications.

These struggles are invariably characterised by intensely destructive aggressive impulses which are often too overwhelming to be felt. To feel them can result in intense depression because the hostility is directed against figures who are still needed and depended upon, however faulty they may be. Furthermore, the hostility is directed at the self inasmuch as there are identifications with the disappointing and hated figures. If the impulse is acted out rather than felt, we can see that the acting-out serves as a defence against depression. This pattern is frequently seen in adolescents who are the offspring of incessantly quarrelling parents, with or without the loss of one or other parent by divorce.

Such adolescents often defend against their depression by adopting a proud, haughty or arrogant façade. To help the adolescent this defence must be confronted with compassion and a capacity to convey to the adolescent, the fact that the helper (nurse, social worker, teacher, therapist or youth group leader) appreciates, respects and understands the need for the character defence. It is particularly difficult to grow and retain this capacity when working with acting-out and violent adolescents because their behaviour can force the parent, teacher, etc. into the role of being punitive, unless or degraded.

Amongst a therapeutic group of adolescents in a hospital setting, there was a change of doctor. The adolescent group attempted to deny any feelings of loss about the previous doctor. They failed to turn up for their group sessions with the new doctor. During the ensuing few weeks there was a continuing atmosphere of generally destructive and unco-operative behaviour which involved not only the therapeutic group but work groups, nursing groups and other hospital activities.

However, eight weeks later several members of the group began to attend the group dressed in funereal clothes, including top hat and black tailcoat and to paint their fingernails black. In the hospital the response to this behaviour was unfortunately a mixture of condemnation, indifference and ridicule. The therapist's interpretation linking the loss of their previous doctor and their anger associated with the new situation was initially ignored. However, when the external appearance and bizarre dress of these adolescents was acknowledged and linked by the therapist to their deep feelings of mourning, the tensions of the group relaxed and the anxieties were contained.

'Treatment'

It is possible to establish some *link* of comparison between the requirements of the psychotherapeutic team on the one hand, and the requirements of parents, teachers and institutions in general on the other, when dealing with adolescents. In both situations, sensitivity, intuition and the capacity to get in touch with some of one's own past adolescent experience is important. It would not be fair to frighten the reader with a long list of prerequisites, but the illustration of the mother-baby relationship may help. Mothers can learn to differentiate crying caused by hunger or physical pain from a demand for attention. Experience becomes mother's ally when she can compare one type of response to another: the way her baby reacts to her if she is feeding him in a quiet atmosphere as compared with one where there are frequent interruptions and noise. But she also learns to understand her infant by another method (which perhaps she is less aware of, but nonetheless it is as effective), and that is, by empathy. If her baby is in pain, feelings of some similar nature in her will probably be evoked, at times without her being consciously aware of them. She can then better imagine how her infant is feeling by putting herself in his place, while at the same time remaining aware of her own identity. This empathy that allows her to be with her baby and enables the baby to feel understood, is the basic mode of understanding and communicating between individuals in any circumstances of life. It is important to stress that this is not a one-way process. Professional workers will add specific theoretical knowledge and skills which enlarge the understanding of certain phenomena, and may develop more sophisticated techniques, but the real matrix of the communication will remain the capacity to empathise with the other.

The treatment of disturbed adolescents could in essence be described as a period of emotional education. By helping them to grow new and more mature ways in coping with an upsurge of new impulse life and at the same time to find better ways of dealing with painful effects and ambivalence towards highly debased and aggrandised inner and outer-objects, the adolescent will hopefully grow towards a more confident independence.

Thus, the purpose of treatment is to promote healthy growth of a kind that will help the adolescent to make his own choice, and to make as full as possible use of his creativity. This process is made difficult because a disturbed adolescent experiences himself either as a reject from society and a failure or as someone grandiosely special who is the victim of a persecutory family and society through no fault of his own. (Parenthetically, it is interesting to note how society can commercialise manifestation of adolescent rebellion e.g. exploiting rebellious adolescent modes of dress, marketing it and perhaps depriving the adolescent of necessary modes of rebellion.)

The extremely rebellious adolescent has great difficulty in believing in the possibility of empathy or understanding between himself and his helpers. He experiences a gap between himself and the staff of a hospital or unit, that is much wider and larger than the ordinary 'generation' gap.

The task of both adolescent and helper is therefore obstructed from the start and very quickly the issue of how to 'control' and help will present itself. This can only be resolved by the growth of a degree of faith on the part of both parties in the value and worth of a relationship which is not a seduction nor an imposition of management. It is in this area where the acting-out of violent and rebellious impulses is likely to put both adult and adolescent to the greatest tests in so far as their belief in the ultimate value of a helping relationship is concerned.

The understanding and discovering more about the inner

conflicts, fears and anxieties of the adolescent, the reasons for his self-destructive, conflict-increasing behaviour, are not always easy to achieve. This type of adolescent feels persecuted by the 'invasion' of understanding adults. To achieve the *rapport* of a trusting relationship can be the therapy of change in itself.

To do this involves adults being real people with adolescent. It involves genuine mutuality, and an ability to identify with the adolescent's predicament, to understand and use his language and help him to appreciate the liberating value of increasing capacity for language, reflection, thought and judgement by offering himself as a flexible yet firm model, for testing against and, later, with.

As Winnicott has said:[7] 'Violence and rebellion can both be seen as a seeking on the part the child for an environmental stability which can stand the strain of his impulsive behaviour. This is the search for an environmental position which has been lost a human attitude which, because it can be relied upon, gives freedom to the individual to move and to act and to get excited.'

It follows from this that benign firmness and strength are important qualities to be sought in adults (parents or staff) who are to work with disturbed adolescents. If these qualities are lacking the search for containment and holding will become more and more desperate and spiral in ever-widening circles. Menzies[8] in her paper 'Growing on two wheels' writes: 'the battle of the generations is fought out on the roads as elswhere and of that perhaps we, as the older generation, are not as understanding as we might be'. Each party in the struggle envies the other and projects its own unresolved and child-parent conflicts on to the other. The adult may over-protect the adolescent or become too permissive or else tend to cut themselves off from the adolescent who by his presence evokes their failure.

Some Concluding Observations

We think it is only possible to relate effectively with adolescents especially in relation to acting-out behaviour, when we are able to evoke something of our own adolescent experience with regard to the feelings contained in such behaviour, and to perceive in it an attempt at communication. There is an enormous difference between meeting the rebelliousness of adolescence and trying to suppress it because the adolescent is striving to find his own identity.

It is important to remember that the turmoil, sometimes communicated abruptly, during adolescence is the expression, whether directly or indirectly of an internal turmoil, which involves rapidly changing social, psychological, physiological processes, the upsurge of sexual and aggressive drives, conflicts over sexual identity and difficulties in establishing an image of oneself as a person in an eternally evolving and complex society such as ours. These problems of adolescence are likely to be much more intense than they would be in a more primitive culture, where roles are often more predetermined and clearly limited, and where expectations are less subject to uncertainty. In recent years there seems to be a more mature type of rebelliousness that manifests itself principally in student movements and political activities. It is quite likely that one could detect acting-out behaviour within these areas, but elements of development and growth are manifested predominantly by more active awareness and participation in the problems which affect society. The adolescent often expresses what adults cannot see—anxiety about the world in which he is going to live as an adult. Adolescents speak a language that needs to be understood: it is not the language of a child and it is not the language of an adult. By misunderstanding it we often produce the acting-out, the rebellion and the violence which we condemn.

REFERENCES

1. S. Freud, *Dora Case* (London, Hogarth Press, 1968), Vol. 7, p. 122.
2. A. Freud, *Problems of Psychoanalytic Technique and Therapy* (London, Hogarth Press and Institute of Psycho-Analysis, 1972), p. 107.
3. C. Rycroft, *A Critical Dictionary of Psycho-analysis* (London, Thomas Nelson and Sons, 1968), p. 1.

4. D. W. Winnicott, *Playing and Reality* (London, Tavistock, 1971), pp. 138–50.
5. A. Main, *Idealisation and Disillusion in Adolescence*, 1969 Winter Lecture (published for The Institute of Psycho-Analysis by Bailliere, Tindall & Cassell).
6. A. Hyatt Williams, *The Risk to Those Who Work with Disturbed Adolescents*, read in Association for the Psychiatric Study of Adolescents, Guildford, 1971.
7. D. W. Winnicott, *Collected Papers* (London, Tavistock, 1958), pp. 306–15.
8. I. Menzies, *The Motor-Cycle: Growing Up on Two Wheels*, 1969 Winter Lecture (published for The Institute of Psycho-Analysis by Bailliere, Tindall & Cassell).

5

Adolescence and Drugs

MARTYN GAY

Introduction

The adolescent drug-taker is generally presented to the public by the mass media as a plague upon our society, never vice versa. The use of drugs to alter psychic states is associated in the public mind with the abuse of hard drugs, and conjures up a picture of adolescents who are continually on the fringes of crime, dropping out from society and becoming dependent upon society for their further care and treatment. These inaccurate images tend to prevent any real understanding of the actual reason for drug abuse among a small minority of adolescents today.

To understand the adolescent drug-taker, we must be prepared to investigate and identify the underlying problems which lead him to choose to distort or ward off reality with drugs. Today, adolescents and adults in Western society live in a drug orientated culture, from aspirins to sleeping pills, from tranquillisers to the pill. We are all ingesting drugs in greater quantity and variety than ever before.

All the crises of adolescence, the fluidity, intense personal conflicts, narcissism, preoccupation with body changes, inexperience, the desire to experiment and to identify problems, all play into the drug-taking culture. The lures of instant cure, instant perception and instant anything through the taking of mind altering drugs are very tempting for the young person of today.

Some Different Types of Adolescent Drug-Taker

Research evidence indicates that there is a caste system developing in groups of young drug-takers.[1] 'Intellectuals' taking drugs, either alone or in groups, are attempting to evaluate some inner meaning to their existence, while the 'non-intellectual' groups simply trip to get some specific bizarre effect. These groups can be further subdivided into the 'dabblers' (US) or 'chippers' (UK) and the 'users' and the 'heads'. The 'dabblers' and 'chippers' play at drug-taking on a sporadic basis, as something daring to do. The 'user' tends to smoke or take small quantities of drugs for psychological reasons, and as a means of personal satisfaction. He likes to savour the effects of drugs and to consider the mystical implications of his strange new experience. The 'head', on the other hand, is very much more likely to be a drop-out from school or work, a person who finds it difficult to communicate with people in authority, and his life tends to centre around the whole drug-taking scene. He tends to take drugs to try to escape personal problems.

Adolescents may also take drugs to prove that they are flexible and capable of withstanding stressful situations, demonstrating that they can behave beyond the limits of adults. There is a comparison here with dangerous driving, drinking to excess, and all risk-taking behaviour associated with delinquency or even sports. A further group temptation is offered by those who feel that the taking of drugs promotes a greater emotional maturity and intellectual depth through 'having experienced oneself' under the effects of drugs. These rationalisations for drug-taking are presented to the adolescent as a means of proving himself both physically and intellectually. The whole drug-taking scene can have a strong dramatic component, not infrequently ending in tragedy. The feeling of being involved in illicit or taboo practices increases the excitement for the adolescent, and he loses many of his strong, inner controls.

The individual bizarre effects of drug-taking are shown by examples of young people who have jumped to their death from windows during an attempt to flee from an intense internal panic which has overtaken them. A Los Angeles student was killed walking along the freeway, convinced that he was invisible to everybody. A young girl in a London flat dived out of the window, proposed destination the United States, in the firm belief that she could fly.[2]

Drug escalation and contagion are two of the most difficult problems to understand and to combat. The group behaviour involved in the relatively innocent use of cannabis can very often facilitate adolescent associations with others who are involved in more serious drug-taking, leading the adolescent at a very early stage to try anything and everything.[3]

Types of Drugs

There are five major categories of mind-altering drugs with potential for physical, psychological abuse: *narcotics*—painkillers such as heroin and morphine; *sedatives*—such as barbiturates, tranquillisers and alcohol; *stimulants*—such as amphetamines and caffeine; *hallucinogens*—such as LSD, marijana and mescaline; and *solvents*—such as Trilene and glue.

There is sometimes the multiple use of drugs, to experiment and obtain the experience of 'highs' and 'lows' of drug-taking. The mixing of drugs from many groups is often an indication of escalation of drug use, from which escape may be complicated. Mixing is particularly dangerous because of known and unknown hazards, and resort to it indicates underlying thoughtlessness, impulsiveness and egocentric, confused inner attitudes.

Further dangers occur from the black market drugs which are very often laced with other drugs, nocuous or innocuous substances, for financial reasons. The danger also arises from the unknown strength of the particular solution. The adolescent has no way of knowing exactly what he is getting, and he may feel that he is taking a known amount of the drug, and then have sudden and disastrous side-effects from overdosage, or even from underdosage because the drug he had been on was really more potent than believed.

The personal attitudes of the drug-taker are a further important variable in influencing the effects of drugs. The social setting in which he takes the drug also will affect his response.

The extreme variety of response to drugs is a major danger for the adolescent drug-taker. During a pot or LSD session, one individual can become boisterous and aggressive, another amorous, another quiet and withdrawn or depressed. There is no knowing which person in a group may be triggered off into an irreversible psychotic state, or panic attack. This is particularly true of the hallucinogenic drugs.

Adolescents with unstable personalities are known to be likely to develop serious complications from drug-taking, bringing out latent problems or heightening existing ones.

Further dangers come from the effects of withdrawal of the drug from the person's body once they have become addicted. The intensity of the symptons vary with the degree of physical and psychological dependence that the person has developed to that particular drug.

Pregnant girls who are addicted to opiates may find that they give birth to a child who is already addicted, and has to be weaned off the drug. There is now a known association between the taking of LSD in pregnant mothers and the production of chromosomal abnormalities. This can be particularly alarming because of the known association of chromosomal damage with leukaemic syndromes and birth defects.

Epidemiology

The increase in the prevalence of narcotic addiction in Great Britain, and particularly in London, in the 1960s is well-documented.[4,5,6] The percentage of under twenty-year-olds in the statistics of addicts known to the Home Office has increased from 7 per cent in 1963 to 35 per cent in 1966, and was 32 per cent in 1971. It was noted that most of the young addicts were of highly unstable personality with a history of social maladjustment, sociopathic conduct, or delinquency, pre-dating their addiction. Prior to this period, most of the narcotic addicts in Britain were of iaterogenic or therapeutic origin, and over the age of fifty.[7]

The number of narcotic addicts amongst school populations is still very small—approximately 0.5 per cent of the total. The age of initiation to drug-taking appears to be falling, so that narcotic addiction is now becoming a problem of early adolescence as well, and the 'pusher' at primary schools is not an unknown phenomenon.

Pierce James reports and warns of the finding that alcohol misuse is a great problem among the young. In his study with Backhouse in 1969 on fourteen- to sixteen-year-old adolescents in a detention centre, only 11 per cent had experienced soft drugs and a small percentage had taken heroin, compared with over a quarter who had drunk alcohol regularly or excessively.[8]

A survey of the London Borough of Bromley by Randall[9] estimates that there is a 2 per cent incidence of soft drug misuse in the fourteen to twenty-one age group, with a small hard core of heroin addicts. Within a community, this hard core of addicts can very rapidly spread their drug taking habits to others. De'Alarcon[10] likened the spread of heroin abuse within a community to a contagious disease. He was able to show that from one or two sources as many as twenty or thirty future addicts were 'infected'. The studies of Pierce James and D'Orban[11] have disclosed abundant evidence of pre-existing personality instability, social maladjustment and delinquency.

It is well known that the Home Office records of addiction are a considerable underestimate of the problem within Britain, and De'Alarcon and Rathod[12] believe that the figure might be four or more times higher than the acknowledged rate within this particular age group.

American surveys[13] of college students collectively show that about 5 per cent admit to having used LSD, with up to 25 per cent of students using cannabis. Of the LSD users, only about 30 per cent were serious users. The heavily involved drug-users tended to have a lower than average educational attainment, and about 3 to 4 per cent of the total student drug-taking population have major psychiatric problems associated with their drug-taking.[14]

American surveys of the drug problems amongst adolescents and the total population reveal disturbing data much worse than in Britain, severe as it is.

Aetiology

The aetiology of drug abuse can only be understood in the total context of drug use in the society in which it occurs. The most commonly used and abused drugs in European and American culture are alcohol and nicotine. We have an interesting paradox in our conceptions of drink and cigarettes, in that we openly refer to them as 'drugs', but behave towards them as if they were quite harmless. We have amongst us enormous social and health problems with alcohol that are usually overlooked, or dealt with in a token manner by society. We have a much smaller problem with other mind-altering drugs, but we appear to have overreacted to them with a climate of emotionalism and hysteria.

Within our social and educational system, adolescents who are unable to cope drop out due to a variety of mental health problems which often include drug abuse, attempted suicide, alcoholism and delinquent behaviour.

Osnos and Laskowitz[15] identified what they feel are the major personality characteristics of aetiological importance in drug-dependent individuals, and these closely follow the problems needed to be overcome in adolescent development, namely inadequate control of impulses, the avoidance of stress and tensions, an intense desire for immediate and effortless gratification, a disturbed relationship to authority manifested by either total resistance or submission to external direction, and persistent exploitative behaviour. There is no evidence that addicts possess any one particular type of drug-dependent personality, since they manifest a wide range of combinations of personal and social pathologies.

Those adolescents who have suffered severe separations from their parents, particularly before the age of sixteen, are

77

more likely to become addicted to drugs and to have associated problems of delinquency and neurotic illness. Bean[16] highlights the association of early experiences of broken relationships, particularly before the age of fifteen, and the onset of drug abuse in adolescence. But although there is a strong previous history of an association of drug abuse and parental deprivation, most of the studies carried out on adolescents within the community indicate that they are still living with their parents, and the majority of them—approximately 75 per cent—are still in regular employment or regular schooling.[12] While studies of delinquent subcultures of adolescents who are also addicted to drugs show that as little as one third of the adolescents are still living with their parents, a quarter are recorded as of no fixed abode, and the remainder were living mainly with friends.[16]

Hawks *et al.*[17] consider that cigarette-smoking and drug-taking are all part of one continuum within adolescence, and they quote Bynner's analysis[18] of early cigarette-smoking, together with the findings of Backhouse and Pierce James[19], which showed a significant relationship between intense alcohol and cigarette use and the use of other drugs in young people. They further consider that tobacco must be regarded as a drug of escalation, particularly when it is used in heavy quantities in adolescence.[9]

Social class is an important aetiological factor in drug abuse in adolescents. Bean[16] feels that social classes 1, 2 and 5 are overrepresented. This is particularly true for social classes 1 and 2 adolescents, where delinquency is associated with their drug abuse. Kosviner *et al.*[20] have suggested that drug abuse may not be entirely related to the material disadvantages often associated with low social class; but particularly in social classes 1 and 2 adolescents it may be associated with a rejection by them of the middle-class standards of their parents. Louria[21] describes simply and in graphic terms the major aetiological culprits of drug abuse as 'all stemming from the problems of family deterioration and urban blight'.

There appears to be no clear-cut evidence that adolescent drug-takers come from any one particular subgroup in a population, such as a delinquent subculture, or any single social class group who are rejecting adult standards.

Adolescent Behaviour and Abuse

Occasional use by curious adolescents is rarely associated with difficulties. On the milder drugs they may temporarily lose control and engage in antisocial activities. This is closely analogous to the adolescent who becomes drunk for the first time, while the person who regularly smokes pot or uses drugs places himself in a similar position to the alcoholic. In both situations the drug has become a central theme of his existence. His emotional growth and development are impeded because problem-solving, so necessary for adolescent development, is not accomplished; he sees the drug of his choice as becoming the universal solution for all his problems. *But this gradually progresses to the point where just obtaining the drug is his central aim—far from it being a universal solution.*

Many adolescents feel quite helpless in coping with what they see as a perfectly unacceptable internal and external world, so that they choose to alter these worlds by chemical means. They see life as 'boring', and the future as uncertain, due to the many internal conflicts which they have to face which are aroused by sexual anxieties, confusion of identity, feelings of fragmentation of their personality. At times, any change the adolescent can make in his internal or external environment may become acceptable.

Keniston[22] says the adolescent is caught up in a dilemma between the cognitive demands of his external environment where there are extremely few prevailing pressures upon him to become morally responsible, courageous, artistically perceptive, emotionally balanced, or to show more feeling, while at the same time he may be under great internal pressure to show extensive emotional reactions. On the contrary, the greatest pressures tend to be towards becoming unemotional, impersonal, seeing things in quite clear-cut, quantitative numerical forms. In fact, the acquisitive, money-dominated Western society. The adolescent faces increasing pressure to perform well academically and to postpone and delay emotional satisfaction until he is much older, and yet he can clearly see around him many examples proving that the greatest admiration and wealth comes to those who do not always delay their inner impulses.

The younger, vulnerable, and more disturbed adolescents may be overwhelmed by extensive flooding of their senses by advertising, education and social pressure, and the violence of society both at war and at peace. They therefore use drugs as a means of countering their numbing, confusing, depressed and disturbed feelings and strive, through drug-taking, to experience strong new inner feelings. The opportunities of controlling these excessive external pressures are now very limited. Many of the traditional means of sublimation are seen by some adolescents as unacceptable— namely religious faith and political ideologies.

The older adolescent begins to struggle with the problems of interpersonal honesty, and genuineness and identity: of being oneself, without the need to adopt roles and to play games. Some may feel walled off from these 'real' experiences, and hope that hallucinogenic and stimulant drugs will provide the chemical answer which enables them to break out of their repressive shell.

The adolescent of any age who is in a phase of experimenting and testing and rebelling finds it difficult to understand why certain laws lay down that one group of drugs or certain patterns of behaviour are unacceptable. He feels that these prohibitions are conveyed to him as a moral judgement, and is goaded by inconsistent adult attitudes towards drugs.

During adolescence, a young person may—for internal and external reasons—so change his attitude towards life and society that he drops out and becomes a casualty—a victim of the delusion that the way to live life is to avoid it. His use of drugs at this time can be seen as a form of nonconformity. Adult society immediately classifies this form of behaviour with other forms of nonconformity which cannot be tolerated, and invokes the use of criminal law.

Adolescence is a time of exploration, experimentation,

change and revolt. The adolescent sees the adult world as though for the first time. He wishes to discover this further for himself, and not to see the world entirely through the eyes of adults. A certain type of adolescent will refuse to believe what he is told about the dangers and difficulties of the drug world, and demands personal exposure to the real drug world as he sees it so that he may test out the validity of his experiences. There is always a danger, of course, that this search for new experiences may become just more than a simple quest for egocentric sensual pleasure, and the drug scene may exercise tremendous complex, compulsive power over his vulnerabilities at first, and then over his strengths.

Individual Factors

The individual factors within the adolescent's personality which make him prone to drug-taking are closely related to the intrapsychic conflict and the extreme internal confusion with which he is trying to cope. These, coupled with the adolescent's natural tendency towards curiosity, lead him to experiment with new drug situations. He sees drug-taking as a personal challenge which he has to face if he is to overcome his own feelings of inner doubt and confusion. He may also fear that if he does not indulge, and is 'chicken', he may be left out, missing something that others in his peer group have experienced. He may see drug-taking as the way in which he can find meaning for himself as a person, enabling him to grapple with his adolescent identity problems. For the individual, drug-taking can be seen as a way of enabling him to become an adequate and competent part of a secure peer group, and help him overcome strong inner feelings of inadequacy, both social and emotional. This allows him momentarily to overcome feelings of desperate private loneliness and helplessness, and the difficulties of the here and now, the past, and not caring about the future.

Peer group factors can provide at the same time the most supporting and the most devastating experiences for the adolescent. This is particularly noticeable in the North American adolescent ghetto group. The taking of drugs

81

becomes a common bond between members of the group. Drugs originally are taken as a challenge or a dare, and are then continued as a confirmation of the *camaraderie* which exists within the group. In the more sophisticated senior school or university groups, this dare is more covertly presented, to hide the underlying peer group threat of rejection if the adolescent does not take the drug.

Sexual Behaviour and Drugs

The taking of drugs may also enhance the young person's feelings of sexual inadequacy, promoting strong internal fears about sexual identity. The action particularly of the hallucinogenic drugs affects ego defences, lessens inhibitions, and has often been reported as heightening sexuality. This can readily lead to an increased awareness of the possibility of strong homosexual and heterosexual feelings about which the adolescent had previously been unaware. With other drugs, there is a close association between drug-taking and the damping of sexual feelings, which may further heighten inner fears of sexual inadequacy.[23] Some adolescents have been reported as using drugs during sexual behaviour to try to delay or prolong the orgasm. The dangerous practice of 'balling' drugs, particularly amphetamines, involves the absorption of drugs through the genital mucosa, further extending the areas of drug experimentation for the adolescent, namely the method of administration—which may be oral, rectal, vaginal or by injection or inhalation. However, drug-addiction causing impotence and frigidity is well known.

Prevention of Drug Abuse

Programmes of drug prevention which are designed to influence young people about the dangers and abuses of drug-taking require very careful preparation and implementation. Many young people are extremely sophisticated about the drugs in use. They are not impressed by comments from those who have very little experience of the current drug scene. There is a strong subculture of jargon and adopted attitudes about drug-taking, and the adolescent is always very suspicious of 'square' information supplied from 'official sources'.

There is however only a limited amount of accurate knowledge about the effects of drugs upon young people, and the news media presentation of the drug scene is often highly distorted. There is a danger that through the circulation of glamorised information we are tending to create a climate of emotionalism and hysteria which works against any effort to try and deal effectively with the problem of drug abuse.

A community mental health approach stressing education, research and prevention is needed. Too much insistence upon stricter controls for drug use as the only effective means of prevention is a guaranteed way of alienating the adolescent. This will often serve as an inducement rather than a discouragement to the taking of drugs.

Highly contradictory messages are put out by adult society and these tend to confuse rather than to help the adolescents. They feel that many of the legal strictures placed upon drug use are questionable, and that they are based upon unsound criteria. They feel that the prohibitions and controls should be constantly re-evaluated and brought up to date in the light of recent research knowledge. When they find that a particular legal sanction is associated with what they feel to be a perfectly harmless drug-taking situation, there is an obvious chance for them to test out their views against adult society. Unfortunately, they often find themselves in the difficult situation of being condemned for drug-taking by the very people who themselves take large quantities of nicotine and alcohol.

The preventive task must include improving the quality of personal, familial and social life. A broadly-based educational programme is necessary for the young adolescent to prepare him for the dangers of drug abuse, and inform him constructively of the resources available if he gets into difficulties. The programme must be geared towards the specific adolescent population being confronted, and special attention must be given to identifying high-risk groups of adolescents, in terms of age and personality difficulties. There is an increasing demand for more informal consultation services from those who are on the fringe of the drug-taking scene, within schools and universities and work groups.

Management and Treatment of the Adolescent Addict

Encouraging the young adolescent to give up his drug-taking habit is not easy. They can receive help compulsorily or voluntarily in clinics, hostels, hospitals, community homes, Borstals or prisons. Certain authorities in the field of drug treatment feel that the treatment programme should be offered in an abstinence-type therapeutic community where the addict is sent to a hospital or hostel rather than to a jail. However, there is always the difficulty of stopping the addict back-sliding once his compulsory or voluntary withdrawal programme is completed, and overcoming his underlying psychological need to continue taking drugs.

Since 1970, in Great Britain a number of special drug treatment centres have been opened. As well as the more institutionally based outpatient clinics and hospital units, there are individual self-help programmes within the community, run by people who themselves have been addicts (e.g. Alcoholics Anonymous, Synanon, Phoenix House).[24] Others are run by groups of highly motivated professional and lay people who are prepared to work on the streets or in hostels for alcoholics or addicts. These facilities provide first-aid help which enables the addicts to dry out and overcome their immediate crises. During this stage the addict is encouraged to accept longer-term intermediate treatment, involving a specially-designed drug addiction treatment programme in hostels or other institutions run by the organisations.

A teamwork approach to the treatment and management of the adolescent addict is the most satisfactory way of helping him and his family. There are many complicated legal, educational, social, moral and religious issues tied up with the management of drug-taking, and all of these must be considered concurrently.

During the early stages of acute intoxication, the adoles-

84

cent requires physical protection. Together with this, appropriate meaures are instituted for the correction of any physical illness or malnutrition. In the writer's opinion, complete cessation of drug-taking is necessary. A number of treatment programmes have been based upon the prolonged withdrawal of drugs, but most of these have run into difficulties in the early stages. Other have made attempts to use the substitution of substances which would cure the original addiction, e.g. Methadone, the chemical substitute for use in the withdrawal treatment of heroin and morphine addiction. This has itself now developed its own pattern of addiction Heroin was originally used in the treatment of opium addiction!

Once the physical state of the patient is restored, and the major physical withdrawal symptoms have been counteracted by the provision of sedative drugs, the more difficut of overcoming the psychological dependence of the young person is tackled. There are invariably serious underlying personality problems, severe neurotic conflicts, or psychotic reactions to assess and treat. The task of the psychotherapist at this stage is to help the adolescent patient with these problems at both a conscious and unconcious level (notably deep emotional dependency, weaning conflicts and severe identity anxieties).

Throughout the treatment programme, the patient's parents will need considerable help with their feelings of helplessness, guilt, anger and blame about having an adolescent who has a drug problem. The families need help to look at their contribution to the addict's problem and to help his reintegration back into society. They must prepare a new emotional environment for him, either at home or supported by them within a self-help group in the community, or encourage him to become sufficiently independent.

In the final stages of treatment, intense work within the community is necessary to elicit long-term supportive resources to ensure that the patient does not feel rejected and alienated when he returns to society. The success or failure of any treatment programme, whether based in a hostel, hospital or private institution, depends *almost entirely upon the success of the follow-up and after-care programme* provided for the drug-taker and his family by the treatment agency.

Treatment and rehabilitation therefore require concerted teamwork and community support, together with continuing support from the patient's family. There is evidence put forward by some that with or without treatment an addict may mature out of his dependence on drugs, but the odds against this are fairly strong.[25] The roots of his insecurity and immaturity which led him to drugs in the first place go deep into his adolescent processes, and still deeper into processes of his childhood.

In the final analysis, the total abstinence from drug-taking can be the only measure of real improvement. The success of treatment depends on individual, cultural, and social factors, the full extent of which are not fully understood at the present time.

The use of mind-altering drugs in adolescence is analogous to playing chemical Russian roulette. The resultant 'ego death' has certain correlates with spontaneously occurring transcendental states, the difference being that from a drugged state you may never come back from the brink of emotional death to experience life again in its fullest form.

REFERENCES

1. E. R. Bloomquist, 'Marijuana: Social Benefit or Social Detriment?' *California Medicine*, Vol. 106 (1967), pp. 246–353.
2. J. P. Smith, 'LSD – The False Illusion', *Federal Drug Administration Papers* (July–August 1967).
3. WHO, *Report on Drug Dependence* (Bulletin, WHO, 1965).
4. T. H. Bewley, 'Heroin Addiction in the United Kingdom', *Brit. Med. J.*, Vol. 2 (1965), pp. 1284–6.
5. T. H. Bewley, O. Ben-Arie and I. P. James, 'Survey of Heroin Addicts Known to the Home Office', *Brit. Med. J.*, Vol. 1 (1968), pp. 725–7.
6. I. Pierce James, 'The Changing Pattern of Narcotic Addiction in Britain, 1959–1969', *Int. J. of Addictions*, Vol. 6, No. 1 (1971), pp. 119–34.
7. H. B. Spear, 'The Growth of Heroin Addiction in the United Kingdom', *Brit. J. Addict.*, Vol. 64 (1969), pp. 245–55.

8. C. I. Backhouse and I. Pierce James, 'The Relationship and Prevalence of Smoking, Drinking and Drug-taking in (delinquent) Adolescent Boys', *Brit. J. Addict.*, Vol. 64 (1969), pp. 75–9.

9. S. Randall, *Drugs in Your Town. Bromley, UK* (Bromley Council of Social Services, 1969).

10. R. De'Alarcon, 'The Spread of Heroin Abuse in a Community', *Bulletin on Narcotics*, Vol. 21, No. 3 (1969), pp. 17–22.

11. I. Pierce James and P. D'Orban, 'Patterns of Delinquency among British Heroin Addicts', *Bulletin on Narcotics*, Vol. 22, No. 2 (1970), pp. 13–19.

12. R. De'Alarcon and N. H. Rathod, 'Prevalence and Early Detection of Heroin Abuse', *Brit. Med. J.*, Vol. 2 (1968), pp. 549–53.

13. S. F. Yolles, *Recent Research on LSD, Marihuana and Other Dangerous Drugs* (NIMH Statement to CHE Juvenile Delinquency, US Senate, 1968).

14. G. D. Klee, 'Drugs and American Youth. Drug Awareness', *Drug Education Activities*, Horman and Fox (eds) (Phila. Penna., Temple University, 1969).

15. R. Osnos and D. Laskowitz, 'A Counselling Centre for Drug Addicts', *Bulletin of Narcotic Drugs*, Vol. 18, No. 4 (1966), pp. 31.

16. P. Bean, 'Social Apsects of Drug Abuse: A Study of London Drug Offenders', *J. Criminal Law Crim. Pol. Sci.*, Vol. 62. No. 1 (1971), pp. 80–6.

17. D. V. Hawks, A. C. Ogborn and M. C. Mitcheson, 'The Strategy of Epidemiological Research in Drug Dependence', *Brit. J. Addict.*, Vol. 65 (1970), 363–8.

18. J. M. Bynner, *The Young Smoker*, (London, HMSO, 1969).

19. C. I. Backhouse and I. Pierce James, 'Dependency Habits in Delinquent Adolescents', *Brit. J. Addict.*, Vol. 64 (1970), pp. 417–18.

20. A. Kosviner, M. Mitcheson, K. Kyers, A. Ogborne, G. V. Stimson, J. Zacune and G. Edwards. 'Heroin Use in a Provincial Town', *The Lancet*, Vol. 1 (1968), pp. 1189.

21. D. B. Louria, 'Some Aspects of the Current Drug Scene, with Emphasis on Drugs in use by Adolescents', *Paediatrics*. Vol. 42, No. 6 (1968), pp. 904–11.

22. K. Keniston, *Drug Use and Student Values* (Nat. Assoc. Student Personnel Administration, Drug Education Project, 1966–7.)

23. H. D. Kleber, 'Student Use of Hallucinogens', *J. American College Health Assoc.* Vol. 14 (Dec. 1965), pp. 109–17.

24. E. Ramirez, 'A New Program to Combat Drug Addiction in New York City', *Brit. J. Addict.*, Vol. 63, No. 69 (1968).

25. AMA, *The Crutch That Cripples. Drug Dependence*, (Committee on Alcoholism and Drug Dependence, Council of Mental Health, AMA, 1968).

6

Some Observations on Depression and Suicide in Adolescents

BILL ALLCHIN

Introduction

These observations have been made in the course of twelve years, working, almost exclusively, with adolescent patients. Some of the work was done in London at a clinic specialising in the outpatient treatment of delinquents and at a day-school for maladjusted children and adolescents run by the London Education Authority. A much longer period has been spent at an inpatient unit for thirty boys and girls, a child and family guidance clinic and a hostel for fourteen boys of working age, all in the south of England. Some of the contacts have been short, no more than one or two sessions. Others have been intensive, and have lasted for a number of years.

My standpoint is based on what is broadly termed 'depth psychology', with more precise formulations in terms of Jung's psychology, particularly as it conceives of ego development, the relationship of ego and self and the basic theory of archetypes.

The attempted emphasis, in my contact with patients, has been an existential one, trying to feel my way into the other person's experience and to understand his or her mode of being in the world. This means respecting his experience, and being concerned with the accurate and detailed description of it. It means trying to get on to the knife-edge of immediate experience, and feeling together the here-and-now of the transference and countertransference situation. This provides a way of trying to grip on to the unpredictable developments of the treatment situation and of accepting that the outcome is unknown. This feeling has been described by Mailer as follows: 'Existential experience, which is to say experience sufficiently unusual so that you don't know how it is going to turn out. You don't know whether you're going to be dead or alive at the end of it, wanted or rejected, cheered or derided. . . . But the hoodlum is more likely to encounter existential experience than the university man.'[1]

It is impossible to imagine any understanding of depression at whatever age it is experienced without reference to the work of the psychoanalysts, and in particular to the classic paper on Mourning and Melancholia by S. Freud, which stands as a primary illumination.[2]

The work that can be done with patients, and its possible outcome, are determined, not only by the skill and persistence of patient and therapist, but also by the economic and social arrangements which influence the location of meeting, the duration of time spent together, and the availability of additional means of help if these are required. This might entail finding a place in an adolescent unit, or a hostel, arranging emergency admission to a psychiatric hospital or drawing into the therapeutic scheme other significant people.

And as young people themselves are so vulnerable to social and economic pressures, so the work with them can never become artificially detached from the wider context in which political and cultural forces also operate.

Development Aspects

Getting through the period of adolescence, say, from the years of twelve to twenty, puts to the test all the developmental progress that has been made up to that point. It shows up areas of failure as well. Speaking of the anatomy of

89

the mental personality Freud observed: 'where pathology displays a break or cleft, under normal conditions there may be a link. If we throw a crystal to the ground it breaks, but it does not break haphazardly; in accordance with the lines of cleavage it falls into fragments, whose limits were already determined by the structure of the crystal although they were invisible.'[3]

Good primary care, in the absence of genetic defect, is the only sure starting point. As Klein puts it: 'The good internalised object is thus one of the preconditions for an integrated and stable ego and for good object relations.'[4]

Such a basis and what can then be built upon it is of crucial importance where the experiencing and mastering of depression is concerned. States of ego weakness may make the task an impossible one. Progress into adolescence implies a lessening of the connection with parents and the struggle to establish alternative sources of affective supply, either from within or without. Significant adults outside the family, friends and the peer group now have to support the developing ego, and to carry helpful projections from the self. Here, then, the stage of lessening of ties with home merges into that of the making of a personal identity. Special difficulties are present for boys, whose experience of a good father may have been absent, either because of death, or desertion of the home. In some cases, the father has been ineffective as a person and unable to counterbalance the influence of a more dominant mother. Neumann has summarised this:

'Even although at the beginning, the all-embracing and directing mother always represents the self, later there is a different development for girls and for boys. The sex-correlation of the self remains feminine for a girl, while for the boy it must be detached from the mother. This crisis of self-discovery is naturally connected with the detachment of the child from the primary relationship.'[5]

This critical process of detachment and the uncertainty of other sources of affective supplies leaves the young person, particularly in early adolescence, prone to rapid mood swings and with little or no reserve supply. These adolescent mood changes are well known, and they may be steep and severe, even if most of them are short-lived. It is not uncommon for an adolescent to feel such a loss of good feeling, or to feel depressed, to the extent that they wish that they had never been born, although the feeling may not last for more than half-an-hour.

Those who have suffered the early loss of a parent or have experienced the break-up of the home may not be able to assimilate the feelings of depression and will be especially open to further mood changes in that direction. In this connection it is perhaps, relevant to mention the stages of separation, described by Bowlby as protest, despair and detachment. So the loss experience and the depression has also an element of rage and anger in it. Sometimes this is turned inwards and exacerbates the depression. Sometimes it issues as aggressive and destructive behaviour.

It is useful to try to differentiate between the experience and handling of a depression for an adolescent who has had good primary care, and those who have suffered long-term emotional deprivation. With the latter group, who make only tenuous contact with adults or peer group, there may be efforts to generate a kind of excitement whose purpose must be to keep at bay the feelings of loss and rage. Such feelings may overwhelm the weak ego and lead to serious self-injury or actual self-destruction.

When the adolescent ego is thus threatened, with consequent heightening of anxiety, there may be an experience of depersonalisation, or loss of sense of being; this may be relieved by motor behaviour of some kind and in severe cases the infliction of pain or self-injury is discovered to be an effective way of restoring a sense of personal reality. Rosenthal, Rinzler, Walsh and Klausner bring this out in a paper describing the wrist-cutting syndrome.[6] Depression was the most common symptom of the group of twenty-four female wrist-cutters who were studied, and the authors speak of 'the final common pathway' of mounting anxiety leading to depersonalisation. They concluded that wrist-cutting was employed as a means of reintegration. For some a degree of pain seemed necessary, for others the sight of blood or of the gaping wound. Each of these acts, they concluded, could be seen as a primitive way of combating the feelings of unreality and emptiness.

Depression in adolescence, then, has as its background the fundamental but natural loss experience of moving away from the safety of childhood, or as a despair at leaving behind the possibility of a happy and safe childhood which was never realised. Because never properly possessed and lived through, the grieving for its passing must necessarily be shot through with ambivalent and angry feelings. Failure to establish new sources of feeling supplies leaves the young person in a sort of emotional vacuum, and there may be a further sense of loss if a sense of identity and social significance fails to develop. Feelings of loss include lack of self-confidence and self-esteem and inability to take setback and disappointment. As a solution, delinquent behaviour, an active attempt to make up a loss, may be seen as more hopeful than passivity, and identification with the criminal subculture provides a ready-made identity. The hard-drug using underworld may meet some of these needs in a similar way.

Adolescents who lack the experience of good primary care, who never had the life in an intact family, with the satisfactory inbuilding of parental figures, will be at special risk in a society which is itself in an unstable and divided condition, and whose institutions can provide such poor help for those whose family life and early years have failed them.

The Nature of the Depression and its Equivalents

Adolescent symptomatology is well known to be varied and unpredictably changeable. Clear cases of deep and stable depressive states as might be seen in adults, have been reported, but are said to be rare, during the period of adolescence. In these, depression manifests itself in the expected way with physical, emotional, intellectual and social effects, which do not require further description here. However, much more typically in young people, depression is not so obvious. The range of symptoms is not so consistent. There may be sleep disturbance, or eating problems, or other somatic complaints. Complaint may be made of loss of interest, or inability to concentrate, or boredom and fatigue. Rapid mood swings and irritability may be seen as well as lack of all motivation, which may go over into passive resistance. Often the young person cannot experience the depression for what it is, nor put his subjective experience into words. Then his actual behaviour may have to speak of his condition. And here there seems to be a value in the idea of the depressive equivalent. These may be various but the point has been made by Mastropaolo[7] that the equivalent must be based on a depressive psychopathology, and the clinical manifestations derive from that, although their characteristics are not in themselves depressive. Among the most common of these behavioural equivalents would appear to be running away from home or wandering, stealing, and some instances of sexual promiscuity or destructive behaviour. The type of stealing concerned would be that described by Rich[8] as the comforting type, which correlates highly with maternal rejection or deprivation. This manifests itself early in life often in stealing from mother. It may occur in any of the socio-economic groups and tends to spread out beyond the family circle. It may persist through adolescence, when it becomes a more consciously elaborated activity, with the secondary gain element obvious, and the depression more deeply hidden. Its characteristics differentiate it from the categories of marauding or proving offences of stealing which Rich described. Such stealing is usually accompanied by lying. Mostly, the stealers themselves disapprove of the act, and certainly fear disapproval or punishment by others. But the mistake of seeing the lying as a piece of immoral behaviour, instead of as a defensive manoeuvre is often still made, and criticism of the stealer along these lines can only lead to further despair and withdrawal. The underlying depression is itself exacerbated, so that, inevitably, more stealing and more lying are promoted. The objects stolen may be those belonging to a person from whom the patient would hope to obtain supplies of an emotional kind, or else from someone who has been chosen as a target, or kind of lightening conductor, on whom to discharge something of the disappointment, rage, or resentment which will have accumulated over the years of deprivation.

Social maladjustment or failure may also be evidence of depression, and in adolescents will apppear as academic failure, or as playing truant. Later it shows as inability to find or to hold a job. It may express itself as failure to develop relationships, leading to increasing loneliness and isolation. As with stealing, all these other manifestations may be met by responses which do not take into account its basis in depression, and thus tend to drive the patient more deeply into it.

In later adolescence, the depression may be experienced as boredom, or disillusionment with life itself, and may be based on a more subtle loss of a sense of value, meaning or purpose in life, which reduces the person himself to a state of meaninglessness and emptiness. There will be apathy, and loss of motivation, and apparently no reason even to try to make contact with anyone who offers help. Such an individual crisis may itself link up with the prevailing emotional climate of the community in which he or she lives. Existing in such a philosophical vacuum may lead some young people into drug-taking, and others into various forms of religious quest.

In adult patients suffering with severe depression there is sometimes a clear link between suicidal and homicidal acts. So, too, in adolescence aggression against self and others may be a depressive equivalent. The acts themselves may range from the trivial and minor acts of destruction which wear away at the physical and mental fabric of an adolescent unit, to dangerous acts of fire-setting, suicide or murder. In the context of the fluidity of adolescent symptomatology, and bearing in mind the problems of recognising the depression, it is obvious that any behaviour of this kind will need careful assessment and attention.

Suicidal Behaviour

Because of the dread of death, contemplation of the suicidal act can arouse a high level of anxiety. Particularly is this so, for the fear and urge to self-destruction which is made explicit by the patient or young person is also in myself, and others. It is understandable that from a religious viewpoint the act is sinful, or from society's angle, clearly antisocial. The act is a devastating critique of the world as the person has up to that point experienced it, and especially in terms of the interpersonal relationships, or the lack of them. Thus, with young people, the suicidal act or threat seems to be aimed especially at the parents, and would seem to set the seal on their essential failure as parents, to transmit the will and capacity to live to the next generation. This being so, even the threat of suicide exercises a leverage on a situation in a way which few other acts or threats can do.

Suicidal attempts and gestures far outnumber acts of self-destruction in the adolescent age group. In older age groups the proportion of self-killings is much higher. Attempts may be made by swallowing small numbers of aspirins or other tablets or by making superficial scratches on one or both wrists or arms. More serious acts may even succeed in self-destruction, even though this is not consciously intended. It is now obvious to us that many acts which fall short of self-destruction have a definite meaning in terms of signalling distress and making an urgent appeal for help. This suggests a desperate need to communicate, and to make an impact on those around who must seem to be unresponsive to the efforts at communication which have already been made. Hence adolescents use more active and telling ways, including hanging, drowning, jumping from buildings or trains, or by shooting. In adults it seems that on the whole the suicidal method is quieter, more passive and more successful in terms of ending life. The more bizarre and unexpected suicidal acts are suggestive of schizophrenic-like states rather than depressive ones, and some may be connected with gross disturbances in the psychosexual sphere. In some of these, however, death may be the accidental outcome of some experimental sadomasochistic behaviour.

Social and cultural factors affect the choice of method, and the wider availability of firearms would obviously lead to a greater use of them for suicidal behaviour. The motor-car is widely available and probably often used. The personality traits of those people with a history of multiple road crashes would certainly overlap with those who make impulsive suicidal attempts. Some motor-cycle crashes, with excessive risk-taking, may also be connected with the idea of the depressive equivalent, and black leather jackets painted with death-heads and gloomy slogans seem to underline the point. For some of these riders, however, depression may not be the basis. They may in fact be offering a challenge to fate or destiny, to see whether one is to live in a meaningful way or perish by one's own hand. Such behaviour often occurs within the context of strong group influences and so needs to be evaluated in terms of the value systems of those groups. More consciously self-destructive acts may also prove contagious, and groups of disturbed adolescents living together are vulnerable to such epidemics. And it would probably be true to say that the larger the group living together, the greater the danger of such infection spreading. For this reason, among others, it is good that the size of adolescent units being developed in the UK seems to be limiting itself to between twenty and forty patients, irrespective of economic considerations. Matthews[9] has described an epidemic of self-injurous behaviour in an adolescent unit which involved more than a third of the patients resident in the unit at the time and included boys and girls. Behaviour included wrist-cutting, pin-sticking and swallowing foreign objects. One of the patients involved later died in circumstances suggestive of suicide. Depression was probably the basic link between those involved. Units staffed by psychiatrists and nurses are particularly open to demands for help expressed as illness or self-injury and their prompt and urgent attention to physical wounds could lead to a crescendo of such acts as patients compete with each other for a share in the usually inadequate amount of staff care and time.

96

In view of the nature of the depressive experience in adolescence, and the difficulty in recognising it, there is little cause for surprise that young people make such desperate efforts to communicate about what is happening in them and to them. There does not seem to be a necessary relationship between the severity of the depression and the seriousness of the suicidal behaviour. Even the not-so-serious gesture must be taken as a serious piece of communication. Once a person has for the first time cut their own skin surface, or swallowed something that they believe to be poisonous, then a situation exists in which further acts become more possible. It seems agreed that there is always some warning sign prior to a suicidal act by a young person. Not all leave a note or a letter, but the act is often meant to be communication to a specific person. The family situation is usually deeply involved as an area to which the person directing both the cry for help and the anger.

The suicidal act does now function as a piece of communication and it usually compels a response from the person's environment. The same is true of stealing. But for both kinds of act, the response may not be what the young person hoped for.

Treatment Possibilities

From what has been said already about the genesis of the depressive experience in adolescents, ways of helping them can be rationally deduced. The patient needs to get into communication with someone, and needs to be able to depend on a source of affective supply and ego support, for what may be a long period. Within the containment of such a relationship, the patient's own inner strength, however much or little there may be of it, may be mobilised and steps taken towards the resolution of the depression, in the tempo dictated by the characteristics of the patient's own personality.

In large, overcrowded, understaffed psychiatric hospitals, to which most adults and some adolescents may be admitted, treatment through a significant personal relationship is

97

rarely possible. For most adults the method will be treatment with antidepressive drugs, and if need be, electric shock therapy. The aim will be to achieve recovery and discharge from hospital in as short a period as possible. My impression is that electric shock therapy is sparingly used for adolescent patients, and the administration of antidepressive drugs may be more unpredictable in effect than is thought to be the case with adult patients. The adolescent is, in fact, most likely to be admitted in an acute suicidal crisis. Admission to a special unit for young people may sometimes be possible. It seems to be accepted that such units may allow for higher medical and nursing staff-patient ratios, and that a better range of facilities may be available. Some, therefore, may be able to work through the depression in a therapeutic or healing way. This assumes not only an emphasis on the psychotherapeutic approach but also that this can take place in a fully supportive setting, with adequate care and supervision of a patient who may, at times, be actively suicidal. There will need to be a good range of educational and recreational facilities as and when the patient may be able to make use of them. If the therapy is forced to work back through the equivalents there is likely to be acting-out in the form of stealing, aggressive behaviour or running away. In cases of severe emotional deprivation, any attempt to uncover the primitive rage and terror and despair contained in the depression should only be undertaken if the supporting situation is adequate to cover the need for continuous personal support and presence.

Sometimes it is safer to work more obliquely, recognising and taking into account the depression and deprivation but making the major theme of therapy a process of ego-building in the context of caring and warm relationships. It is rarely possible to undertake treatment on an outpatient basis, with or without the support of drugs, unless the patient can be seen weekly and can tolerate the tension between sessions. And it assumes a good supporting environment, be it the patient's own home, or a hostel or residential home. Adolescents who are admitted to a General Hospital following a suicidal attempt should not be discharged until a proper psychiatric assessment has been made of the patient's own state and of the environment to which it is intended to return him. After a prolonged inpatient admission, adolescents may need a continuing period of after-care and social rehabilitation, and dependency relationships should resolve naturally as the on-going momentum of adolescent development is resumed.

Conclusion

Depression in young people has been shown to be a potentially serious condition. Occurring as it does at a time when psychological development is fast-moving and the ego still of variable strength and degree of integration, it can lead to a period of deep subjective misery and to a slowing of emotional, intellectual and social development. It can involve one or more suicidal attempts and even a successful act of self-destruction. It is not always easy to recognise, and the depressive equivalents in behavioural terms may lead the patient into antisocial behaviour, and entail condemnation by society. The condition is treatable so long as the proper facilities are available. All too often the tag of 'lazy' attached to a depressed young person connotes nothing more or less than laziness and lack of concern on the part of the adults in the immediate environment.

A depressed person may have a depressing effect on others. The condition of emotional depletion implies a demand for an emotional supply and a dependence which may also lead others to a response of withdrawal. Hence depressed patients, especially if they feel much guilt, have a further problem in trying to conceal their feelings. This leads to a further feeling of being cut off from reality and from help. A state of mind containing in it an experience of loss, along with the inevitable anger, also implies a criticism of the world which in some significant way has failed the patient, and may be continuing to fail to respond to a human need.

The diminution of social function in a young person, leading to academic incompetence, loss of motivation, or work incapacity readily generates negative and critical attitudes in

99

others. A hectic and 'driven' social order such as our own has little time or patience for such things. Indeed, the common response to actual bereavement itself is often a desperate effort to carry on with life and work as if 'nothing had happened'. And others reinforce this, with their reluctance to share in sadness and grief. But in a depressive experience, energy is withdrawn into the psyche in order to perform a significant task of inner adaptation and development. The way in which a depression is treated has, therefore, wide and deep repercussions. At present society makes resources available for little more than first-aid. And physical methods of treatment while they may cut short the depression, tend to leave the patient in a continuing state of unknowing about his or her life experience.

Contemporary values and a commercialised culture, with an emphasis on producing and consuming, has little interest in sadness, depression and suffering. If the expectations of life-style, promoted by the mass media, allow for anything, it is for a concept of illness, whether physical or mental, which sees treatment as no more than the readjustment or repair of a mechanism. And for this the person submits passively to the attention of the professional and objective expert. The same procedure is followed with a malfunctioning motor-car, refrigerator or computer. Thus a crisis, or turning point in life, loses its significance and meaning. The aim seems to be the rapid return of the producer/consumer to the firing line.

But depression as an experience of predominant and sometimes devastating mood change requires intensive and sometimes prolonged care in order that its negativity can be made to yield up the fruits of its hidden opposite. Thus, the social and cultural view of depression and suicide must have a continuing influence on the treatment of people within society. Such a problem has been put concisely by a poet, a young man, in the following way: 'What the persistent apple-cheeked optimism that's for ever showing off its biceps does for a community is to demobilise and disintegrate it. Whereas a clean, honest, unsentimental sadness, for all its helpless airs, does urge us forward, creating with its fragile hands, the greatest spiritual treasures of mankind.'[10]

BIBLIOGRAPHY

1. N. Mailer, 'Talking of Violence' *Twentieth Century*, Vol. 173, No. 1024 (1964–5), p. 109.
2. S. Freud, *Mourning and Melancholia. Collected Papers*, Vol. 4 (London 1925).
3. S. Freud, *New Introductory Lectures* (London, Hogarth Press, 1933), p. 80.
4. M. Klein, *On Identification. New Directions in Psycho-Analysis* (London, Tavistock, 1955), p. 312.
5. E. Neumann, *Current Trends in Analytical Psychology* (London, Tavistock, 1961), p. 51.
6. R. J. Rosenthal, C. Rinzler, R. Walsh, E. Klausner, 'Wrist-Cutting Syndrome', *American Journal of Psychiatry*, Vol. 128 (1972), pp. 1363–8.
7. C. Mastropaolo, *Depressive States in Childhood and Adolescence*, A. L. Annell (ed.) (Stockholm, 1972), p. 290.
8. J. Rich, 'Types of Stealing', *The Lancet* (21 April, 1956), p. 496.
9. P. C. Matthews, 'Epidemic Injury in an Adolescent Unit', *International Journal of Social Psychiatry*, Vol. 14 (1968), p. 125.
10. Y. Yevtushenko, *A Precocious Autobiography* (Harmondsworth, Penguin Books, 1965), p. 77.

7

Adolescence and Individual Treatment

JOHN BYNG-HALL

Introduction

Adolescents can, as is well known, create a number of thorny problems for any adults who encounter them. Therapists are not exempt. The art of therapy lies in the way in which these difficulties are negotiated. Adolescents require varying degrees of emotional distance from adults in order to complete the transition to adulthood; they have to establish their own separate but related identities, find their sexual relationships outside the home and establish sufficient autonomy to be able to fend for themselves. This transition is not achieved through a steady progression, but with many swings, often of breathtaking speed from the world of children to that of strutting, arrogant young adults, and back again. Thus the grown-up, including the therapist, may find himself being treated in rapid succession as: the parent held responsible for his every action, peer and ally, grandparent, authority bogey man, understanding uncle, or out of touch grown-up; at times emulated, at others made the villain whose every value automatically defines the youngster's anti-value system.

Disturbed youngsters may get stuck in any of these postures or may have so many conflicts with adults that they cannot use these various modes of relating for growth. When the

102

relationship with an adult provides what is identified as treatment, which is the case in psychotherapy, a whole new set of ideas and attitudes are added. These need to be considered before moving on to consider the process of treatment.

Concept of Illness

What is it that takes an adolescent into treatment? It is not something that happens easily. The degree of distress experienced either by the adolescent or by those around him is often considerable. Help from an outside expert may be sought if the difficulty is not sorted out by the individual or by his family. In searching for a remedy the family might start to conceptualise the problem as an illness, especially if it is difficult to understand. This then mobilises a number of deeply ingrained attitudes and expectations. People expect to take a pain to a doctor, who will then diagnose an illness within them, prescribe the right treatment, which, if they do as they are told, should cure the illness. This has a number of disadvantages when applied to emotional difficulties. The image of a doctor who knows the answers and tells the patient what to do may be dangerously inviting to one in whom the crucial struggle to take responsibility for what is happening feels overwhelmingly difficult.

There is another problem for adolescents in particular. The illness concept when applied to the mind, that is mental illness, invokes ideas of something foreign, strange, mad and perhaps out of control. Adolescents are often stirred by powerful feelings which they cannot fully understand, and which often seem out of control. There cannot be many adolescents who have not, at some time or other, entertained the idea of madness. Some families, perplexed by what is happening, may also have their suspicions. Referring a young person to a psychiatric clinic can fill them all with anxiety. One of the developmental tasks of an adolescent is to crystalise an identity. Part of the image of madness may become incorporated into the adolescent's own sense of identity and into the family's view of him. This may compound any loss of sense of reality which might actually be occurring. Once the mental illness label has become attached, the adolescent's own observations of reality may be discounted. It is assumed that he does not understand and so he is often left in the dark by the others. All these things can happen before a doctor is involved. The doctor is then under pressure to confirm the diagnosis. Admission to a mental hospital is an especially powerful way of confirming the label of mental illness. Dr R. D. Scott[1] describes how the perception of an emotional problem as an 'illness' in an individual prevents perception of the problem's interpersonal roots and hence closes the possibilities of doing anything about it.

Adolescents are particularly likely to be used as scapegoats by families. Bell and Vogel[2] discuss the role of the disturbed child as diverting from stresses within the marriage, thus sacrificing himself to keep the family intact. R. D. Laing[3] has portrayed the intolerable position into which schizophrenic patients are placed by their families. There is also increasing awareness that difficulties in a family may be a symptom of a wider difficulty within society itself. Thus there is, rightly, a growing dissatisfaction with a focus on a symptom in an individual without reference to the context in which it occurs.

The implications of the swing away from the individual focus needs, however, to be thought out. It is very easy merely to reverse the manoeuvre: the individual can blame his environment for his difficulties and thus evade responsibility for his own actions. Unless the adolescent, in particular, accepts the challenge of responsibility for controlling himself, he will remain a slave to his own impulses. The clinician who wittingly or unwittingly conveys to an adolescent the notion that he is just a victim of his family or environment may rob him of his greatest asset, the experience of choice. Because the balance in capacity to change rests more with the youngster than his parents, this potential must not be wasted. It is hard for an adolescent to give up a grievance when he feels it has been justified by the clinician.

As the medical model for therapy becomes modified the best of the old should be assimilated into a new model. Caring and concern can be mobilised by the concept of illness. The youngster may be seen as meriting help rather than as deliberately tiresome. In this way also hostility towards the 'patient' may be held in check. (This may be of more than academic interest: adolescents can arouse murderous fury.) The difficulty with this apparent gain is that it is related to and probably springs from an attitude found in parents of young children. Temper tantrums and other awkward behaviour can be tolerated, say, in a toddler by making allowance for his age. 'Oh well, we have to expect this, he is only three.' This becomes, 'Oh well, we have to expect this, he is ill.' Adolescents are very sensitive to infantilising attitudes. They would prefer to have their anger and the message it contains taken seriously, although it can nevertheless be reassuring to find that their fury can be tolerated.

The concept of illness can provide the basis for a therapeutic alliance. The therapist and the patient can get together in a non-judgemental way to try to remove the 'sick', and hence foreign, behaviour. Medical ethics provide an already existing setting in which confidentiality is respected; there is licence to discuss bodies and their sexual functions; professional conduct has defined ethical standards; and professional responsibility has roots both in social structure and in academic traditions. The adolescent may feel freer to discuss things that are important to him in this setting, although, goodness knows, it can still be difficult enough.

Many of the valuable aspects of this tradition have already been embraced by non-medical therapists. There is at present an interesting state of flux in which the care of human distress is carried by many professional groups. As this chapter is entitled 'treatment' the medical model has to be discussed. It is easy to forget its presence and the many ramifications which are important for adolescents. The power of the model is more pervasive than many of us would care to admit.

Who Is Complaining, and About What?

This book is about adolescents. The reader is likely to be interested in those situations where the symptoms, or distress, for which treatment is sought, is somehow centred on the adolescent. The complaining may be done either by those in the adolescent's environment, or by the young person himself; and sometimes by both. Adults are more likely to take on the complaining role on behalf of younger adolescents, but as he grows older the young person increasingly takes the responsibility for seeking help himself.

There are however some situations in which, whatever the age, the pain is felt more by others, than by the adolescent. This may happen when the adolescent cannot bear to experience any feelings of distress. He may then dissipate the experience through uncontrolled action, often aggressive or sexual. If the intolerable pain comes from a feeling of deprivation, stealing may occur, or he may obliterate it with drugs. Adolescents often deny distress by adopting a belligerent 'I could not care less' attitude. If the adolescent withdraws, fails to function properly or behaves strangely, those around him are likely to be upset and seek help for him.

As the adolescent becomes more able to experience distress and see it as his own, rather than as a persecution coming from outside, he is more likely to want to ask for help. He may feel depressed or anxious or become dissatisfied with the way he relates, especially towards members of the opposite sex.

Whereas an achieved sense of self-identity roots people within a niche they feel they know in a world experienced as knowable, the exciting search for self that the adolescent undertakes gains richness from his capacity to loosen the reins of old models and to experiment with new. There may be times however when the self seems to disintegrate with confusion or into a terrifying void. These periods may intermingle with the sense of madness mentioned earlier. Boundaries with what others might come to call madness or psychosis may become hard to discern.

There are two views of crises, in particular those of confusion of identity, appearing in an adolescent. One is a widely-held view that the psychosocial changes which occur in adolescents produce crisis situations, and hence difficulties that erupt in adolescence frequently represent a normal, often transitory phenomenon. This view has been challenged by some authors such as Masterson[4] who found that certain symptoms appearing in an experimental group of adolescents were still present later in life. Whichever way this debate will eventually be resolved the issue of treatment remains crucial. The high capacity to adapt and grow is one hallmark of adolescence. This provides a fruitful opportunity for intervention, before difficulties become fixed.

Another great hallmark of adolescence is the tendency to provide its own solutions. Many adolescents are creative, but taking drugs to obliterate psychic pain or boredom, plus opting out, are prevalent styles which worry the adult world. The challenge to the caring profession is to find creative ways of linking with adolescents. This should go hand in hand with a careful reappraisal of how the therapist's own approach can make the situation worse, e.g. those with a medical or para-medical background need to examine the misuse of the medical model. It is also important for them to consider whether it is not a short step from the idea that every pain and stress must be countered by the signing of a prescription for drugs, to that of self-administration of drugs.

Setting Up Treatment Facilities

The guiding principles of treatment ultimately have to be pragmatic. Who can change? What is possible? Which techniques are available and what effects do they produce?

The traditional role of the clinician is to offer his service to those who want it. With adolescents, as we have seen, it is frequently others who want the treatment to be given to a youngster who did not seek it himself. Every therapist is delighted when an adolescent does ask for help for himself because this can produce such a fruitful relationship with the therapist. Some clinics go out of their way to make self-referral easy—say, by arranging for walk-in facilities which

107

allow the young person to make contact exactly when he is ready and avoid the hurdle of referral procedures.

Although the adolescent's positive motivation is valuable it does not preclude useful work if it is absent. One example is the adolescent who is committed to a penal institution. Work can be done by exploring how he feels about being pushed around, for instance into the psychiatrists's office, against his will. The next question to explore is why has this happened to him, of all the possible people in the world? This is the relevant issue, and part of him probably knows it. When the adolescent is sent by his family, the clinician is aware that however much he is in need of help there may well be another aspect to the referral; this is the adolescent's role as scapegoat for the family. If the problem is seen as all within the adolescent, this automatically defines the others as without problems. There are two approaches clinicians can make to this. One is for the adolescent to be offered individual help for himself, while the parents are invited to see someone else whose role will be to help unravel some of their own difficulties, in the hopes that this will reduce their need to provoke the adolescent back into the scapegoat role should his symptom subside. Other clinicians take the view that seeing the adolescent on his own powerfully confirms his role as patient and hence as scapegoat, and enables the rest of the family to avoid change. The adolescent himself may not be allowed to change in this situation. Beall[5] describes how the acceptance of the family's definition of who is the problem may establish what she calls a 'false contract'. To avoid this she recommends seeing the whole family together, initially, in order to define the real problems and set up appropriate treatment contracts with the right people. This would seem appropriate when there is lack of evidence that the adolescent is seeking help in his own right. Even if he is taking the initiative a family group is still an important part of assessment, although it may be advisable to see him on his own at first to discuss his feelings about the family group. He may only be able to engage in treatment if he feels that it is not directly related to his parents.

Inpatient Treatment

Starting with the family group is particularly important when the form of treatment being contemplated for the adolescent is admission to a mental hospital, which is, as has been mentioned, a particularly potent way of attaching the label of mental illness. In a paper by Bruggen, Byng-Hall and Pitt-Aikins[6] a unit for younger adolescents is described which uses the technique of meeting the family first as out-patients. A reason for admission, which is understood by all, including the adolescent, is sought in the family meeting. The only reason which, in the long run, makes sense out of a choice of inpatient rather than outpatient treatment, is that the adolescent cannot be coped with or managed at home. The staff ask what is happening in the family, who is finding what painful, and is the situation intolerable? A number of advantages follow from this approach. The family-coping mechanisms become the focus of attention. Therapy can be directed, prior to admission, towards removing those diffi-culties which produce the wish for a separation. In this way a significant number of admissions are avoided. In those families in which the adolescent is admitted because the situation has reached levels intolerable to the family, family therapy continues with the same focus, thus working towards reducing family conflict and hence facilitating reunion. Admission becomes quite short.

The reason for admission is not the diagnosis of an illness, a task for doctors, but the presence of one particular symptom 'the child cannot be coped with at home'. The parents are the ones who know whether this is true or not. In this way they can take responsibility for deciding about admission and discharge. Very frequently it is the break-down of parental authority producing an 'out of control' adolescent, which is central to the need for separation. Parents are given the task of deciding about admission and subsequently discharge, in a family setting. The therapeutic skills of the staff help the family to unravel the tangles which have undermined the effective wielding of parental authority.

109

These difficulties are often based on a failure of the parents to support each other which is subsequently exploited by the youngster, As these mechanisms become apparent, and are understood, parents, especially apparently passive fathers, may emerge with a surprising degree of fresh assertion.

Family as Patient

As the symptom is 'cannot be coped with at home' the problem is defined as a shared one. Cure involves parents learning to cope plus child becoming easier to manage. The medical model has changed from an illness in one person to a sick set of family relationships: the family as 'patient'. The two models have parallel features; individuals in the family are like different organs of an ill person. The symptom of a physical illness may centre in one place, say an upset stomach, but treatment must take into account the whole person; he will not recover if ordinary demands are made on the rest of him. He needs to be in bed until the vomiting stops. Treatment needs to take the family into account although one person may still receive the main attention, just as medicine specifically for the stomach may be required, in addition to bed rest.

The model of the 'family as patient' removes the main objection to the illness model, namely its capacity to support scapegoating manoeuvres, by identifying an autonomous illness process in an individual.

Outpatient Treatment

In an outpatient setting treatment plans can include family therapy (which will be discussed in the next chapter), or treating subunits of the family. This, of course, includes treatment of the individual adolescent on his own, with or without his parents being seen at the same time, depending on how enmeshed the adolescent is within his family. Age is obviously one of the factors deciding this.

Treatment techniques available for individuals include psychotherapy, psychoanalysis, behaviour therapy, brief counselling or physical forms of treatment such as medication. He may also be given group psychotherapy, with his peers as opposed to his family. Clearly there is insufficient space to describe all these techniques. Psychotherapy with the individual will now be considered briefly. A more thorough description can be found in Holmes[7] and Lorand and Schneer.[8]

Treatment of the Individual

Therapeutic alliance

The therapist's first task is to establish a therapeutic alliance with the adolescent. This presents a rather complicated distancing problem. The clinician needs to ally himself with the coping, more adult, aspect of the adolescent in the common task of understanding and changing that part of the patient which is giving trouble. Thus one aspect of the relationship is close; but this 'therapy team' then stands back to look at how the 'patient' part is behaving, in order to provide some distance within the adolescent between the sense of the self as he would like to be, and the troubled or alien part which he may want to change. The sense of confidence and trust within the 'therapy team' provides the adolescent with the feeling that he can, in time, gain control of himself. This sense of eventual self-mastery can be extremely reassuring because many, particularly younger, adolescents are terrified by the way in which their aggressive and sexual urges pull them into an uncontrollable whirlwind of risky action and experience. The therapeutic alliance is therefore a very precious commodity. It has, however, many obstacles to overcome. The young person often has problems in his relationship with adults. He may be keeping the grown-ups at a distance because of a dreaded pull back to childhood which he tries to avoid; or he may be feeling persecuted by the maelstrom of feelings inside, which he deals with by perceiving as attacks coming from outside. An adult might arouse anxiety because of the sexual feelings which occur in what is felt to be an incestuous context (in relation to the therapist too). All these different feelings come up within the conflict between the adolescent and the series of images of adults, mostly shadows of parents, which the adolescent now perceives in the therapist. This transference of past images on to the therapist provides an opportunity, in the setting of the therapeutic alliance, to understand and work through some of the unresolved difficulties.

Example of individual treatment

George illustrates vividly some of the major challenges, discomforts and rich rewards of working with disturbed adolescents. He was fifteen when he was first seen at a school for delinquent boys. He was the son of a prostitute, his father was unknown. He had been in a children's home until the age of four when he had been adopted by a well meaning middle-aged couple who felt sorry for him when they visited the home. His temper tantrums and soiling, which had been problems in the children's home steadily decreased following the adoption, and he seemed relatively settled and happy during latency. At fourteen he suddenly began to be aggressive to his adoptive parents and to run away from home. He was sent to the school with the diagnosis 'out of parental control'.

At the first meeting he presented himself as a hopeless mess: scruffy, filthy, snotty-nosed, flopping awkwardly in his chair. He seemed initially to be pleased to come, taking it as an opportunity to grouse about the school staff. The therapist explored with him his mixed feelings about coming; his anxiety about being treated as mad; but also how he presented himself as a mess as if asking to be sorted out and cleaned up. Over a few weeks of weekly interviews he seemed to develop some idea of using the sessions to understand why he got into the muddles that he did. He then became increasingly angry with the school staff, in particular the headmaster who referred him. The therapist took this up in two ways. Firstly, that the referral touched on his angry feelings about his parents who passed him on to the home, and also the home who passed him on to his adoptive parents.

The second way was to interpret his anger with the therapist, as he was complaining about the referral specifically to him. For several weeks the latter aspect became the major focus because his behaviour deteriorated in school, which made the master become angry with the therapist. George's anxiety about expressing his anger directly to the therapist was interpreted. Perhaps he felt that the therapist would also throw him out as his adoptive parents had done when he showed them his anger. By messing around in the school he showed the psychiatrist up and the master could then be angry with the psychiatrist on George's behalf.

George began to bring pure, vitriolic, white hot anger to the sessions. He would often stand in the doorway screaming abuse, and leave again after ten minutes, never having come into the room. All the therapist could do, when he was allowed any say, was to suggest that George was anxious about whether the therapist could survive his anger, and that keeping his distance and leaving early was protecting him from it. At other times he would suggest that George was letting him know what it felt like to be abandoned. The therapist felt a great sense of uneasy despair. After a month or two of this extremely uncomfortable situation George was able to come in and sit down. As soon as he seemed capable of listening the therapist risked an interpretation: 'Perhaps it feels as if I am your real father, and that you have been letting me know how angry you were about being abandoned.' The effect of this was startling. George opened his eyes wide, 'How did you know?' The tension immediately eased and it became possible to explore and understand what had been happening. Running away from home had represented an attempt to find his father. He had kept somewhere an idealised image of his unknown father. Although this had preserved something good for George it had increased his disillusionment in his adoptive father at adolescence.

From this point in therapy his relationships improved, both with his parents at weekends and in the school. The sessions were taken up with exploring what choices he had before him, always including the possibility that he could

113

H

choose to make a mess of things, both for himself and the therapist if he felt like it. In practice he got into less and less trouble, started smartening himself up and doing well at work. A completely new person emerged. Everyone was delighted and very surprised.

As it came towards his time to leave the school, therapy returned to his feelings of abandonment. This time sad feelings were included in the experience. His angry, could-not-care-less attitude turned out to hide profound sadness and despair. He misbehaved a few times although not seriously. The therapist interpreted this behaviour as a communication from that part of George which wanted to stay; an attempt to prove that he needed sorting out. He eventually left for a job as originally planned, a year after therapy started.

This piece of therapy is introduced here because it illustrates fairly clear-cut phases and processes. Most therapy is more complex and less dramatic both in the intensity of expression of feelings and the sharp watershed of improvement.

Beginning therapy

The feelings about the referral need to be taken up in the first session, especially those about being mad, or being thought of as crazy. An art is also required in managing the balance between work with negative and positive feelings. If the therapist fails to acknowledge or deal with the hostility early on, it can lead to a superficial engagement which quickly breaks down when the angry feelings openly flood in. On the other hand, a therapist who talks mainly about the youngster's anger, before trust or warmth is sufficiently established, can be felt to be persecuting. This can also lead to a breaking off treatment. It may, nevertheless, be unwise to openly acknowledge the closeness. The youngster arrives full of angry complaints that he does not want, or need, to come. In this way he keeps an image of himself as having grown out of all that kid stuff, despite the fact that his wish for help has been expressed by coming.

In George's case it seemed important that he was able to establish some links before his anger poured out in all its intensity. A reasonable relationship with his adoptive parents during latency may have enabled him to do this.

Process of therapy

The adolescent brings with him various unresolved feelings and attitudes, many unconscious, based on painful experiences with past figures. These are then transferred to the therapist who in phantasy becomes like these past figures. This provides an opportunity to re-experience the old conflict and resolve it in the new relationship. George put the therapist in the role of a number of his past figures and was able to find that feelings could be expressed without the unconsciously anticipated catastrophic outcomes.

The therapist's interventions are aimed at bringing the unconscious material into awareness and providing the patient with the possibility of doing something about it, instead of remaining propelled by unknown inner drives.

One mechanism that frequently leads to failure to resolve conflict is the tendency to divide the target of feelings into 'good' and 'bad' people. To focus one's inner hatred on a 'bad' person enables one to protect good feelings about other people important to one. This is based on a phantasy that the angry feelings will destroy the loved person, and so the hatred has to be directed away from them, and from the inner images representing them.

In George's case this led to difficulties. Adolescence set him on the search for his identity and, hence, for the real parents, especially father, inside himself. To avoid his huge anger with his real parents from obliterating the 'good' image he had built up of his father, he directed his anger at his adoptive parents and set off to look for his real father. Therapy helped him to experience the mixed loving and hating feelings to one person, the therapist, who survived and tolerated it without retaliation. This probably helped him to start relating again, with mixed feelings, to his adoptive parents, the people who in reality had been good to him.

Younger adolescents often find it impossible to hold their intense feelings inside themselves. They may dissipate them through action. Another way of ridding themselves of uncomfortable feelings is to make other people, especially parental figures, experience the same conflicting feelings. As it is now the grown-ups' problem they can go off relieved. This may mean that they fail to learn how to resolve the conflict unless the adult helps them to take back the problem.

The therapist, through George's abuse and premature departures from sessions, became filled with George's conflict—angry despair—but held it inside himself without resorting to angry running off, which was George's solution. When George could tolerate it, the therapist put it back to him in understandable form so that he could integrate the painful clash of feelings. It is as if the patient's intolerable feelings pass into the therapist who contains them by struggling to understand them. When they are more sorted out they can be passed back to the patient. Much of therapy is based on this mechanism.

Termination

Terminating therapy provides invaluable opportunities for working at relevant problems for adolescents. After all, their task is to leave parental figures. George had past separation problems and worked through some of them; at this point he experienced and owned some of his despair.

Because leaving adults is developmentally appropriate it is often hard to know whether adolescents terminating therapy on their own initiative is a growth experience, or merely avoiding resolution of a problem. In practice, whatever the therapist's plans are for long-term treatment, adolescents tend, on average, to leave quite quickly. It is important to recognise this. Useful work can be done surprisingly quickly. An assumption that there is plenty of time can leave important issues on the shelf. Psychotherapists working with adolescents need to devise techniques for brief intervention. The relevant issues need to be isolated and focused on. The

116

steady unfolding of every problem in its own time, possible with adults, is often not feasible. Some youngsters have such deep-seated problems, however, that a short period in therapy will leave them untouched. Thus the setting for therapy needs to be considered at the outset. George would have left too quickly if he had not had the holding environment of the school; as it was, a year seemed all too short.

Termination with George was fairly typical. The therapist felt sad at the parting, and he was left feeling worried about certain important areas that had been largely untouched, such as George's relationship with women. He wondered how George would fare with girl friends. Perhaps parents often feel like this as their offspring launch out into the world. When is it better to hold them back for more growth, when is it better to let them go?

The Older Adolescent

The treatment alliance with late adolescents or young adults, say of student age, can be based on a maturer footing. It becomes more of a joint venture with the patient increasingly working things out for himself. Words and concepts are used increasingly in the search for values and identity. The real need for each generation to work out its own image, plus the idealism of young people can give therapy a sense of exploration with even a poetic quality to it.

People in this period of their lives have the advantage of flexibility and growth, the potential for which may diminish in later years. A therapeutic relationship still contains, however, the potential fury related to a feeling that the patient is being treated as a child. This tends to provoke a rising crescendo of scornful belittling of the therapist, relegating him, as it were, to the second childhood of stupid senility. There is then very little room for anxiety about who is childish and who is mature. The therapist needs to rescue the creative potential within the omnipotence from its purely defensive use in dealing with anxiety about babyishness. A rearguard action directed against disallowed infantile feelings can use

117

up the energy which could otherwise be harnessed in the forward and outward drive of idealism.

The therapist can help the patient to discover that the destructive, greedy, helpless feelings which may have been walled off in childhood, can be re-experienced and re-owned in relationship to the therapist without the feared dire consequences. The warmth, aliveness and the capacity to enjoy, which are such a rich part of babyhood may be made more readily available to the young person.

REFERENCES

1. R. D. Scott, 'The Treatment Barrier: I' *British Journal of Medical Psychology*, Vol. 46 (1973).
2. E. F. Vogel and N. W. Bell, 'The Emotionally Disturbed Child as the Family Scapegoat', Chapter 31 in *A Modern Introduction to the Family*, revised edition, N. W. Bell and E. F. Vogel (eds), (New York, The Free Press; and London, Collier, Macmillan, 1968), pp. 412–27.
3. R. D. Laing and A. Esterson, *Sanity, Madness and the Family; Families of Schizophrenics* (London, Tavistock, 1964).
4. J. F. Masterson, 'The Symptomatic Adolescent Five Years Later: He Didn't Grow Out of It', *American Journal of Psychiatry*, Vol. 123 (1967), pp. 1338–45.
5. L. Beall, 'The Corrupt Contract: Problems in Conjoint Therapy with Parents and Children', *American Journal of Orthopsychiatry*, Vol. 42 (1972), pp. 77–81.
6. P. Bruggen, J. Byng-Hall and T. Pitt-Aikens, 'The Reason for Admission as a Focus of Work for an Adolescent Unit', *British Journal of Psychiatry*, Vol. 122 (1973), pp. 319–29.
7. D. J. Holmes, *The Adolescent in Psychotherapy* (Boston, Little, Brown; London, J. and A. Churchill, 1964).
8. S. Lorand and H. Shneer (eds), *Adolescents: Psychoanalytic Approach to Problems and Therapy* (New York, Hoeber, 1962).

8

Conjoint Family Therapy

JOHN BYNG-HALL

When one or more therapists venture to work with a whole family in the same room it is called conjoint family therapy. For the therapists, who are confronted with the complexities and pressures of family life, this kind of treatment is often exciting, at times disturbing, and usually fascinating—reaching, as it does, into the centre of human relationships. In an attempt to keep theory and practice together this chapter will begin by following one family through treatment and then some principles of technique will be extracted.

The O'Malley family consisted of both parents plus Mary, aged twenty-four and James, fourteen. They came to the clinic because James, although intelligent and potentially of university calibre, was bottom of his class. Mr O'Malley, a swarthy, red-faced, fifty-five-year-old Irish builder, had come to England thirty-seven years ago following rows with his highly religious Catholic family. He shared the exiled role with his wife who had fallen foul of her Dutch Lutheran father during her late adolescence and had come to Britain to escape.

After an assessment the family was offered fortnightly meetings of one and a half hours each. At the session following this offer, which was also the third family meeting, James entered the room first; he was fair, plump, soft looking, but with a sharp twinkle in his eye. Mother, who followed, was small, round, well wrapped up with coat and scarves. Before the therapists had time to take note of her or Mary, pale and insignificant behind her, father made his presence felt, ushering his family into the room, loudly telling James to hang up his coat. The meeting was in the office of the social worker, Miss A. James sat between her and the male psychiatrist, Dr B. As the parents were seating themselves together on the couch, James turned towards Miss A, looked at the books on her shelf, and remarked that it was a medical fact that women had larger and heavier brains than men. He had read it in a magazine. In the mean-time Mary glided into the seat next to Miss A. The final seating arrangement was with the women in one half of the room, the men in the other; but James seemed to be more a part of the women's group, his back turned to the men.

James's view of the dimensions of the female brain were not challenged by the family, and Miss A was the only one to look enquiringly towards the psychiatrist, Dr B who commented that the whole family seemed to think that women are brainier than men. Miss A pointed out that this was illustrated by the fact that questions were directed towards her. This suggestion was checked, and found, in part, to be felt to be true. Mary had a degree in mathematics; mother could speak six languages; father said he thought James was stupid, and as for himself, he was a practical working man, but he had not had any opportunities to learn things. An alternative view emerged which was that mother thought James might possibly be a genius. At this Mr O'Malley became angry and said that she was always spoiling him with such nonsensical ideas; it made James get ideas above his station, he might want to take over. The two male members of the family became engaged in a heated argument which revealed that they were both quick-witted and enjoyed combat. Mrs O'Malley and Mary sat quietly observing the to and fro of the verbal battle. As spectators they played a role in perpetuating the sequence. Dr B tried to intervene to make some comment but because his first words were instantly assumed to be the first salvo of an argument, he soon found himself arguing that he was not arguing. He was caught up in the impelling force of the male tussle.

Much of the rest of the session was taken up in an exploration of the significance of intelligence to this family. It had become equated with femininity. The therapists pointed out that this put James into an impossible position. If he worked hard and successfully, he might then lose assurance of his masculinity. Father said that he hated to see his wife overfeeding his son, making him fat and weak (and, by implication, feminine). The therapists said that they wondered whether the male verbal fighting, in which Dr B had also been caught up, was the family's way of reasserting the masculine role. Father described how when he was James's age he had fought his peers and had been very athletic. He was disgusted with his son. The therapists noted to themselves, for future reference, that there seemed also to be a degree of excitement and affection expressed, but simultaneously denied, in the fighting between father and son. They explored the anxiety about James taking over from his father. James might feel anxious about doing better than his father and this might expose his father to the sadness of having missed his own education when, as was obvious, he could have done well. Father in turn seemed to anticipate his son suddenly taking over from him rather than steadily achieving more independence. Perhaps this was due to Mr O'Malley's experiences as a teenager, where his challenge to his father had created so much anxiety on both sides that he had had to leave home.

Family groups offer remarkable opportunities for assessing the essence of a problem. Interpersonal tangles can be seen to fit together in a way which can suddenly make an individual's dilemma quite comprehensible. The therapists felt they could empathise with James's reluctance to learn, but also with father's vulnerability. No doubt their ability to tune into uncomfortable experiences was conveyed to the family. This process of sensing the plight of individual family members while the others are observing can provide a model for the use of empathy as the basis for mutual understanding. Therapists will, whether they like it or not, be used

121

as models by the family. This fact must be kept in mind and utilised. It is easy to forget.

Uncovering personal dilemmas and linking them in a new and meaningful way to the interplay of the family pressures can give the family a sense of a system which has unwittingly become tangled. This may lessen the impression for each that another has deliberately done them down, and hence is the cause of all the pain. The family therapist learns from painful experience how powerfully he can be buffeted himself by disturbed family systems. This can give him a humble appreciation of the human predicament. Such as a non-judgemental attitude must be linked, however, to zeal for devising ways of undoing the various knots.

Some Therapeutic Strategies

The science of change in family relationships is still only young. But this does not excuse the clinician from thinking about, planning, and observing the effects of his interventions. Indeed it makes this work even more important. The diversity of techniques devised by family therapists has been vividly portrayed in a paper by Beels and Ferber.[1]

Among the multitude of approaches some fundamental choices can be made by the therapists. One such possible choice is between the use of understanding as the path to change, on the one hand, and direct attempts to change the family's system of relating and ways of doing things, on the other. The danger of searching for insight is that all the time can be spent contemplating the problem, and not getting down to doing anything about it. On the other hand, to grapple with, and solve, a problem without gaining any idea of why the muddle arose in the first place, may leave the family to fall into a similar trap in the future. There does not necessarily have to be an exclusive choice between working with insight and changing the system; both can, and, should be worked with together. Each technique may be more effective however if the therapist is clear about what he is doing.

In the meeting described earlier, the O'Malley's were invited to try to understand what was happening. The thera-

122

pists used segments of the session to illustrate how what was happening could be understood. In this way, any insight gained could be linked in a direct and personal way to the family system of doing things, possibly giving them a higher potential to change their system for themselves. The therapists, in fact, provide a research model to the family by pausing, examining what has happened, seeing its consequences, and reflecting on its meaning. This model can be taken home and used; the family might start noting how they relate and then wonder why. Such a pattern gives the family time to pause and reflect, reducing the tendency to respond instantaneously to each other, a trait which can so quickly lead to deadlocked, stereotyped patterns of relating. An ability to anticipate consequences may allow the choice of a different action.

At one time the therapists suggested that the parents should discuss between themselves their different views of James's intelligence. This represented a direct attempt to change the family system because the parents usually avoided facing their differences. Those therapists who concentrate exclusively on changing the family system would probably have avoided offering their own understanding of why the parents held these differing views. To do so it might be argued would have merely distracted the parents from their struggle to settle their differences, an essential step if they were to stop giving James conflicting messages about his intelligence. Dr B and Miss A did give their interpretations of why the parents had different views. In this way they conveyed to the family not only that they should actively resolve differences but also that resolution could come through a better understanding of each other.

Understanding may be gained both about the present situation and about how the past influences the present. In telling the therapists about the past a new perspective becomes available to members of the family. To hear afresh, or often for the first time, about a parent's or spouse's early painful experiences can make sense out of behaviour which previously may have seemed merely perverse. Mr O'Malley's extreme difficulty in allowing money to be spent could be more readily forgiven after hearing about his early struggle for survival. Establishing that his present behaviour was linked more closely to the past than to the present helped the family to insist on planning with the present economic realities more in mind.

Much useful work can be done to help the family relate more appropriately. Often it becomes abundantly clear that communications within the family have become tangled, producing much suffering through the ensuing misunderstandings. People frequently respond to the internal image that they have of another person, without bothering to check this against what he actually feels and thinks. A common warning that this is happening is given when people start to speak *for* each other. The therapist can, in that situation, encourage people to speak for themselves. Some therapists make their major technique that of clarifying communications, leaving the meanings behind the communications to take care of themselves. The therapists can also help the family to be more sensitively and accurately aware of the feelings both in themselves and others. For instance, depression is often seen as anger, irritability or laziness, or denied through exaggerated excitement and over-activity. Once the distress has been recognised members can relate more sympathetically to each other. The underlying causes of the depression can then be sought. As depression may also be a more appropriate affect in the setting of what family members are doing to each other, the experience of a sense of remorse may be a step in taking responsibility for the situation. The family can be helped to be more aware of hidden themes which emerge in the sessions, say covert denigration of others, where sugary sweet politeness is the overt activity. Often the hidden theme subtly dominates the situation, and is likely to continue to do so if it remains beyond awareness.

Any outsider has the advantage of being able to see some things that the family, blinded by its own proximity, cannot. The therapist is in a particularly privileged position because any family engaged actively in therapy will be communicating, sometimes unwittingly, fundamental facts about itself, often with startling clarity and speed. This can be surprising to a therapist who is used to working with individuals, in which he painstakingly builds up a picture over what is often a long period of time. Because the diagnostic picture of a family can be painted so quickly and vividly, it is possible to share understanding with the family quickly as well. By using material from everyday important relationships, the therapist has a feeling that his work is directly and profoundly relevant. Many clinicians who try family therapy become extremely enthusiastic, especially about the speed and degree of change that it seems to produce. Despite this potential for change which the family group provides, the therapist will also become humbly aware of the power that some family groups have to resist any attempts to change them.

For the first few months the O'Malleys seemed to be using therapy, and changing. After about nine months, however, the sessions became very stereotyped with well-worn patterns of interaction established. James had started to get better results at school but these were always played down by every member of the family. A typical sequence would be, Mr O'Malley: 'Now, James, you have been using us. You are the only one who brings us here.' Mrs O'Malley and Mary look at James. James: 'Dad, you know jolly well that it is you who forced us to come today.' Mr O'Malley (getting red and angry): 'It is only because you are lazy that we have to come. You drag us here. You. . . .' Mrs O'Malley nods in assent. Dr B: 'It seems as if James is in an impossible situation again. He has to be seen to be lazy as the only way of getting you all here.' Miss A to James: 'Perhaps that's why you have to play down your improved results!' And so on. Despite all the therapists' various attempts to shift the situation, the old rituals would be repeated endlessly.

Here another basic decision about strategy has to be taken. Some centres may choose to capitalise on the rapid changes which can occur, by excluding those that do not show early signs of changing, and stopping when other families reach stagnant periods, but offering further contact should they want it later. If the clinic wants to tackle the problem of rigid family systems then it needs to explore concepts which can explain the low adaptability of some families both prior to and during treatment. Therapeutic strategies to promote change can then be planned in the light of these ideas. The success of the interventions should then be considered.

Rigid Family Patterns Produced by Mutual Defence

The theory of mutual defence has been discussed in *Adolescence* Chapter 4. In essence the theory is that each individual's defensive needs are met by a repeated overt family drama which denies and hides what each individual fears most. Thus the outer drama which is played out is often the opposite to, or in contrast to, what is most feared. For example, the family in which never an angry word is exchanged may be made up of individuals who are terrified of their inner fury and hence the family myth of 'we are always nice to each other' is felt to be necessary to avoid a family scene of destructive violence. Thus if the family has a rule against overt anger it provides a mutual defence for all members. There may however be a high price to pay in anger expressed in covert devious ways, and in failure of the functioning of creative assertive anger.

Patterns of mutual defence are initiated in the marriage. The O'Malley's marriage seemed to have provided two basic defensive requirements. Each came to marriage with a need to establish a relationship which would not break down. This need was based on painful, unhealed experiences of family disintegration after angry disagreements over religion. They found in each other kindred spirits who had repudiated religion altogether and, what is more, each had thrown over a religion which was potentially at loggerheads with his own. Thus on the face of it there seemed to be a double assurance that religious disagreements, whether over purity or heresy, would not split them apart. They adopted the shared view that they understood and agreed with each other perfectly; there were no barriers between them. In short there was no difference between them. This assumption controlled and hid their absolutely fundamental differences which might have boiled up and burst them asunder. Although religion had in their adolescence provided the context for the family rows, the difficulty stemmed from each parent's early childhood. The pain of separating from their mothers had been avoided by refusing to recognise that people were separate individuals and hence they felt that they could always know automatically what the others were thinking—that after all it was the same as their own thoughts. This mechanism had broken down when, as adolescents, they were driven to find separate identities, and hence to refute this assumption. Thus one type of mutual defence is based on sharing a similar defensive manoeuvre.

The second mutual defence was based on the playing of opposite roles. In one session they described their first meeting. Mother had slipped and fallen half-way down a cliff, father had rescued her. From that moment mother had seemed to father to be a soft helpless person, a reflection of the soft part of himself which he had to repudiate because of its associations with homosexuality. To mother, father seemed like a tough rescuing dominant male, a reflection of her own disallowed masculine potential. Thus each represented the rejected part of the other and the marriage provided a way of reassuring themselves of their feminine and masculine roles. The overt drama was a very masculine man dominating a passive wife. This hid and controlled the overt feared drama of a powerful woman pushing her weak husband around. It will be noted that, paradoxically, this fits neatly into the other defence of 'perfect understanding'. Mother felt she could tune directly into Mr O'Malley's masculinity and father felt the same way about his perception of Mrs O'Malley's femininity.

Children have to be incorporated into the defensive manoeuvre if it is to remain a viable defence. Mary fitted well into the ethos of quiet, submissive, intelligent femininity: a confirmation for mother of her own femininity, again reflecting perfect harmony between the two. Difficulties showed only when Mary failed to leave home to go to university, and had to live at home. She had no relationships outside the home. As a child James fitted snugly into the role of the boisterous boy. He never worked at school, thus confirming for father the role of lively, 'brawn better than brain' masculinity. The problem started for a number of reasons in adolescence. He was providing differing needs for his parents. He was conceived in the parents' forties partly in order to keep mother feeling young; to bolster her maternal image. For her he needed to stay a baby, but for father he was required to live an adventurous hypermasculine role. These two demands led to conflict with a compromise solution; he remained fat and babyish for mother and had verbal rather than physical fights with father. As we have already seen, he found it impossible to use his brain. Interestingly, however, he was fascinated by, and good at, religious knowledge—in particular of the reformation period. It is not hard to see why this was so.

Much space has been given to outlining the family pathology and the underlying theory. This was necessary in order to understand the therapeutic impasses and the strategies that were employed. The whole of the above description was pieced together with the family over the two years of therapy. How and when this was done needs further elaboration.

Resistance to Change

When a family comes to therapy they are partly wanting to change, to break down defences, but there will also be the opposite drive to shore them up again. Defences are, after all, used for some reason.

The art of therapy lies in establishing a sufficiently strong therapeutic alliance for the family to feel safe enough to let go a little, and then steering a course which neither asks for too much change nor allows futile stagnation. The family can rapidly leave treatment, as every family therapist knows, if this balance is not correct.

The family's equilibrium is already likely to have been upset and this has caused enough pain to ask for help. If it is the adolescent who is seen as the patient, it is he who has frequently been instrumental in upsetting the family homeostasis. He may have challenged the family's defensive posture. When he does this he risks being seen as ill, or mad, or at least as the only one with a problem. In this way the other members of the family can continue their denial of difficulties within themselves. The therapists will be pressurised into confirming this through diagnosing and treating the illness within the adolescent. The rest of the family may feel that it is coming merely in order to help the therapists to treat the adolescent. This view may be held on to, sometimes secretly, even if they overtly agree that it is a family problem and accept family therapy. The O'Malley family were, it will be remembered, quite open about placing the problem in James. It will be noted that he colluded with this view by denying the academic progress that he had made. Sometimes working with the interactions, demonstrating the way in which each person plays a part in the conflicts can be enough to take the focus off the adolescent. In other situations many hours of work have to be done to delineate the function that the adolescent's symptoms play within the family, before this defensive position can be given up.

The question can be asked: what would happen if the symptom was not available? Whenever Mr and Mrs O'Malley started to disagree, James would interrupt with the inevitable result that they would come together to concentrate on James's difficulty again. The therapists demonstrated this process to the family and tried to explore why all members of the family seemed so afraid of the parents airing their differences. They also pointed out that there was a price to pay if they were never allowed a chance to resolve any difficulties. Despite all these and many other techniques, which the therapists often felt were basically correct, the stereotyped family interactions continued. This made the therapists explore other functions of the system.

One fascinating aspect of the presenting problem is that it is frequently produced through a compromise between the need for expression of the family problem and the attempt to avoid it. The resulting symptom meets both needs. If the family is, say, defending itself against taboo incestuous sexuality within the home, an adolescent may become publicly promiscuous outside, thus everyone in the family can

129

I

become preoccupied with sexuality out there, diverting attention from what is happening within. Applying this principle soon made sense of James's symptom, and the current therapeutic impasse. The whole family's inability to learn from the therapists was hidden by the preoccupation with James's learning difficulties. This diversionary technique was so successful that the therapists took some time to see the therapeutic log-jam in these terms, although they knew that learning patterns are influenced by family styles. The therapists pointed out the shared nature of the learning difficulties. This had the effect of loosening the system for a while, but then it jammed once again.

Therapists Recruited into Mutual Defence Patterns

Mutual defence in families is based on establishing a social structure which enables individual members to avoid what they cannot tolerate. The mutually acceptable pattern of relationships is achieved by reaching an equilibrium between the pressures to recruit others into suitable roles and the ability and willingness to fit those prescribed roles. The point at which negotiation stops is when the established pattern successfully allows all members to be unaware of any intolerable difficulties. Further change is then likely to be experienced as painful, and hence to be avoided. To maintain the integrity of the defensive matrix there will be attempts to recruit the therapists into roles where shared blind areas can once again provide sanctuary against demands for painful change. This recruiting process can be very powerful. Therapists can be amazed, when they listen to tape-recordings of sessions, to see how they were caught up in certain activities and hence failed to see other quite obvious themes. With experience this difficulty becomes less pronounced, but whatever the experience of the therapists, various safeguards can, and should if possible, be used. If the therapist can minimise his own personal blind-spots through therapy for himself, it reduces his potential for colluding with families. However successful this is, he is still likely to be blinkered at times. Co-therapy, that is, using two therapists, can further reduce the blind areas. Discussion after the session between the therapists then becomes vital, because the two therapists' relationship to each other can become part of the defensive social matrix, and can block further change. The tangles that the co-therapists get into with each other often reflect important conflicts within the family. An examination of these difficulties can give diagnostic information. But even with discussion immediately after the session, common blank areas remain. A third person, or alternatively a group of practising family therapists, may often see the tangles more clearly. They can service the therapy.

The volume of data in a family session is so great that it is impossible for the therapists to notice everything that occurs. This may partly explain why avoided areas can be so successfully hidden. Tape, or preferably videotape, recordings can provide invaluable opportunities for exploring the details of the group process, thus widening the therapists' field of perception. Considerable trust between the therapists and those helping them is needed. When one of the aims is to discover where the therapists missed the point there is a high potential for the therapists to feel criticised. If the servicing of the therapy is done through a joint exploration of the recording, the very real nature of the difficulties can be appreciated by all. It also provides a good setting for working out in practical detail what might be done in future in similar circumstances.

The therapists explored with the O'Malley family how they continually complained about James's refusal to do school homework. On the other hand, they themselves never discussed the sessions at home; they never did their therapy homework. James turned to the therapists and asked whether they did any homework. Perhaps this question was prompted by the fact that the therapeutic intervention had become stereotyped. The therapists were not learning new ways of dealing with the family. Miss A and Dr B met afterwards somewhat shamefacedly to discuss why, despite espousing the philosophy of servicing therapy they had never managed to meet regularly, or to arrange for a third helper.

The answer that emerged was that they both felt that they understood each other well anyway, despite the fact that they had never worked together before. They could recognise Mr and Mrs O'Malley's illusion of sameness in this view. They then looked beyond this assumption to find that underneath they did have disagreements. Dr B felt that Miss A was too allied to James and spent too much time supporting his achievements. This, he felt, pushed father further into criticising James, and anyway James needed to learn to value himself. Miss A felt Dr B to be critical of James, which left her feeling alone in her task of supporting this vulnerable, but talented boy. To air these differences, they had felt, might break up what was otherwise a nicely working team.

They then recognised that Mr and Mrs O'Malley polarised in a similar way in their attitudes to James despite their claim to agree over everything. If the therapists behaved as pale reflections of the parents, no wonder change did not occur. After this the therapists become more flexible in their approach and more perceptive of the family dynamics. It was after this that most of the work was done in helping the family to see why and how they defended themselves against anxieties over differing, and against any doubts whatsoever about heterosexuality. The part each was playing to support these defences was acknowledged, but the cost then counted. The parents deprived themselves of the growing, learning, creative relationship with which they could enjoy their middle and late years. The children were unable to leave home or feel secure enough in their identities to mature sexually.

A Second Chance to Grow Away from Parental Figures

Therapists, in particular co-therapy teams consisting of a man and a woman, are likely to attract feelings that originated in relation to the grandparents. This happened with the O'Malleys, in particular those feelings related to autonomy and leaving home. Both parents, perhaps mainly Mr O'Malley, worked through many of their unresolved feelings towards their parents in the relationship to Dr B and Miss A.

Mr O'Malley was angry at times, wanting to leave therapy; at other times he was obsequious and compliant. Once when Dr B was away ill he sat in Dr B's chair saying that he was now going to be in charge. Difficulties always increased when the therapists had a holiday break. Early in therapy most feelings had to be channelled through James, who expressed them for his parents. For instance, he expressed the ambivalence about coming by, on the one hand, retaining his symptom which kept them coming as well as taking the initiative in arranging the next session, but on the other hand openly saying that he did not want to come and that it was not helping. As his parents were helped to express their feelings more openly towards the therapists, he was freed from this role. Father became the next main spokesman for ambivalence. He was openly furious with the therapists but continued coming nevertheless. Mother remained quiet. Mr O'Malley's role of defending her against having to express her own angry feelings was clarified. Mrs O'Malley's and the others' anxiety lest open anger should lead to their dismissal was interpreted by the therapists. Mrs O'Malley then started to say that she thought that it was all a load of rubbish and proceeded to miss two sessions, but returned. Thereafter she used silence less for purposes of controlling the group. The parents had some rows for the first time ever (they said). The earlier suggestion that they should thrash things out together may only now have become possible as they discovered that it was safe to express mixed feelings. The therapists were not thanked for this at the time, but held responsible for the conflict until right at the end of treatment when they could see that to have survived a period when disagreements seemed to be threatening a break-up provided the marriage with a real, as opposed to a mythical, sense of security.

Termination

Working towards ending therapy can produce very fruitful changes. After eighteen months it seemed difficult to envisage the family stopping; although battered by the family on occasions, the therapists had grown curiously fond of them. They recognised that the parents had no model inside themselves of leaving home as a planned, mutually acceptable, steadily-maturing process. They were, as a consequence, unable to support their children in this process. With this in mind the therapists suggested that they should consider stopping the family meetings after another six months. The therapeutic interventions then concentrated on the family's feelings about stopping, the sadness, the anger, and the anxiety.

It was agreed together that it was appropriate for Mary to stop attending at once. She had already largely withdrawn. Father bought her a flat of her own and she left home. Although father still visited her twice a week this represented a major shift in the family system, a new capacity to let go. James was able to get a series of good work marks and admit that he was proud of some of his work.

All contact was not cut off suddenly by the therapists; instead different ways of continuing were discussed and offered. James could see a therapist on his own for his private problems, and his parents could continue to meet Miss A and Dr B for a while. James took up the offer but his parents declined.

Family therapy can provide a very useful base for individual work, as well as being the only offer to some families. James was now well motivated and his disturbance was no longer expressing something for his parents, who were now able to allow him to change. In the last few meetings the family reflected on the experience of therapy. They had felt a big change after the decision to terminate. The major change seemed to be a greater sense of freedom with an improvement in father-son relationship. Mr O'Malley allowed his son more autonomy and James matured considerably. The last meeting was very moving. Father, as he shook hands warmly with Dr B said: 'You know doc I really hated you at one time.'

REFERENCES

1. C. C. Beels and A. Ferber, 'Family Therapy: a view', *Family Process*, Vol. 8 (1969), pp. 280–314.

INDEX

139

Index

therapy *see* psychotherapy
transference 56–7, 89, 112,
  115–16
trauma 16–17, 21, 23

United States of America *see*
  America

verbalisation 56, 58, 64, 93
violence 37–8, 43–8, 50, 54–71
  passim
Vogel, E. F. 104, 118n.

Walsh, R. 91, 101n.
Winnicott, D. W. 36, 39, 59, 69,
  71n.
World Health Organisation 86n.

Yeats, W. B. 54
Yevtushenko, Y. 100, 101n.
Yolles, S. F. 87n.

Zacune, J. 87n.